Collins

My First English-English-Urdu Dictionary

انگریزی - انگریزی - اردو

Collins

My First English–English–Urdu Dictionary

انگریزی - انگریزی - اردو

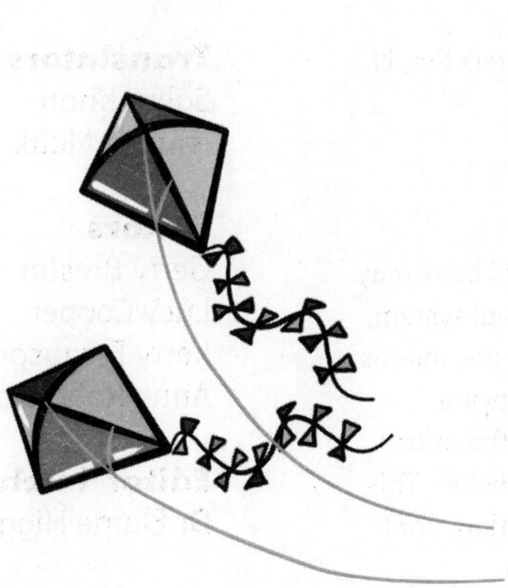

HarperCollins Publishers
Westerhill Road
Bishopbriggs
Glasgow
G64 2QT

First edition 2011
Reprinted Indian edition 2018
Reprint 10 9 8 7 6 5 4 3

ISBN: 978-93-5177-651-2

www.collinslanguage.com

A catalogue record for this book is available from the British Library

Artwork and design by Q2A Media

Printed in India by Saurabh Printers Pvt. Ltd.

Images used under licence from Shutterstock.com

Editorial consultant
Dr Muntazir Qaimi
Senior Linguist, Centre of Indian Languages (CIL), School of Language, Literature and Culture Studies (SLL&CS), Jawaharlal Nehru University, New Delhi

Translation co-ordination
Ajit Shirodkar

Translators
Salim Khan
Ishrath Malik

Editors
Gerry Breslin
Lucy Cooper
Kerry Ferguson
Anne Robertson

Editor-in-chief
Dr Elaine Higgleton

MRP: 231

اس لغت میں کوئی لفظ کیسے تلاش کیا جاتا ہے

ate - axe

ate
⇨ Look at **eat**.
*He **ate** three apples.*

atlas *noun*
atlases
An **atlas** is a book of maps.
ایٹلس، خریطہ

attack *verb*
attacks, attacking, attacked
If someone **attacks** another person, they try to hurt them.
حملہ کرنا

attention *noun*
If you pay **attention**, you watch and listen.
توجہ
*He always pays **attention** in class.*

attract *verb*
attracts, attracting, attracted
If something **attracts** things to it, it makes them move towards it.
راغب کرنا
*Magnets **attract** anything made of iron.*

---

*I put my glass on a red **mat**.*

match *noun*
matches
1 A **match** is a small, thin stick that makes a flame when you rub it on a rough surface.
ماچس کی تیلی
*She lit a **match** and held it up to the candle.*
2 A **match** is a game of football, cricket, or some other sport.
مقابلہ، میچ
*We won all our **matches** last year.*

match *verb*
matches, matching, matched
If one thing **matches** another, they look good together.
مماثل ہونا
*Do these shoes **match** my dress?*

اگر آپ حروف تہجی کے ترتیب سے تمام حروف جانتے ہیں تو لغت دیکھنا آسان ہوگا۔

1. پہلے حرف سے متعلق سوچو اور لغت میں درست صفحات ڈھونڈھنے کے لئے صفحے کے کنارے دیکھو۔
2. دوسرے حرف سے متعلق سوچو اور صفحے کے اوپر کے الفاظ دیکھو تاکہ تم کو جس صفحے کی ضرورت ہے اسے تلاش کرنے میں مدد مل سکے۔
3. اب تم جو لفظ تلاش کرنا چاہتے ہو اس کے لئے صفحے پر الفاظ کی فہرست دیکھو۔
4. تم جانچ کر سکتے ہو کہ الفاظ کی ہجے کیسے کی جاتی ہے۔
5. تم دیکھ سکتے ہو کہ مختلف طریقے سے استعمال کرنے میں الفاظ کس طرح بدلتے ہیں۔
6. تم دیکھ سکتے ہو کہ اس لفظ کے کیا معنی ہوتے ہیں۔
7. تم [اردو] ترجمہ دیکھ سکتے ہو۔
8. تم دیکھ سکتے ہو کہ لفظ کو جملوں میں کس طرح استعمال کیا جاتا ہے۔
9. تم دیکھ سکتے ہو کہ آیا کس لفظ کے ایک سے زیادہ معنی ہیں۔
10. اگر لفظ اسم، فعل یا صفت ہے تو آپ دیکھ سکتے ہیں۔ کچھ الفاظ ایک سے زائد طریقے سے استعمال کئے جا سکتے ہیں۔

الفاظ کس طرح استعمال ہوتے ہیں

فعل

فعل وہ الفاظ ہیں جن سے تم جو کرتے ہو اس کا اظہار ہوتا ہے۔

eat *verb*
cry *verb*
talk *verb*

فعل کو کئی طریقے سے استعمال کیا جاسکتا ہے۔

eats, eating, ate, eaten
cries, crying, cried
talks, talking, talked

فعل کا استعمال ان چیزوں کے بارے میں بات کرنے میں کیا جاسکتا ہے. جو تم اس وقت کررہے ہو۔

*He **teaches** people how to play the piano.*
*He **is** in the school football team.*

ان کا استعمال ان چیزوں سے متعلق بات چیت میں بھی کیا جاسکتا ہے. جو تم نے ماضی میں کی ہیں۔

*She **took** the plates into the kitchen.*
*She **talked** to him on the phone.*

ان کا استعمال ان چیزوں سے متعلق بات چیت کرنے میں بھی کیا جاسکتا ہے. جو آپ مستقبل میں کریں گے۔

*Mum **will** be angry.*
*Our teacher **will** give the prizes to the winners.*
***We'll** come along later.*

اسم

اسم وہ الفاظ ہوتے ہیں جن سے افراد، مقامات اور اشیاء کا اظہار ہوتا ہے۔

arm *noun*
bird *noun*
car *noun*

اگر آپ کے پاس کوئی چیز ایک سے زیادہ ہے تو اس لفظ کے آخر میں **s**- لگاتے ہیں۔

arms
birds
cars

صفت

صفت تم کو یہ بتاتی ہے کہ اشیاء، افراد اور مقامات کس طرح کے ہیں۔

happy *adjective*
wild *adjective*
wet *adjective*

صفت کو کئی طریقے سے استعمال کیا جاسکتا ہے۔

happier, happiest
wilder, wildest
wetter, wettest

ہجوں کا ماہر بننے کے لئے مفید مشورے!

جب آپ کو لغت میں وہ لفظ مل جائے. جو آپ تلاش کررہے ہیں تو اسے "Look, Say, Cover, Write, Check" کے طریقے سے سیکھنے کی کوشش کرو تاکہ یہ جان سکو کہ اس کی ہجے کیسے لکھتے ہیں:

Look لفظ کو غور سے دیکھو۔
اس کی شکل اور سائز دیکھو۔ اس لفظ میں موجود حروف دیکھو تاکہ یہ دیکھ سکو کہ آیا اس میں حروف کسی مخصوص طرز پر ہیں جن سے آپ یاد کرسکیں اور مستقبل میں اس کا املا لکھنے میں آپ کو مدد مل سکے مثلاً bright, light, tight

Say لفظ کو زور سے پڑھو۔
غور کرو کہ اس لفظ سے کیسی آواز نکلتی ہے! کیا آپ کسی ایسے لفظ کی ہجے کرسکتے ہیں جس کی آواز اس لفظ کی طرح نکلتی ہو؟ کیا آپ کے لفظ کی آواز کتاب میں دئے گئے لفظ کی آواز کی طرز پر ہے؟ یہ لفظ بولئے اور اس کی ہجے کرنے کی کوشش کیجئے۔

Cover لفظ کو چھپا لو تاکہ تم اسے دیکھ نہ سکو۔

Write لفظ کو لغت میں دیکھے بغیر لکھو۔ لکھتے ہوئے یہ دیکھو کہ یہ لفظ کیسا نظر آتا ہے! کیا یہ صحیح لگتا ہے؟ کیا اس کی شکل صحیح ہے؟ کیا اس کی لمبائی صحیح ہے؟

Check جانچ کرو کہ یہ لفظ تم نے بالکل صحیح لکھا ہے۔

Aa

abacus *noun*
abacuses

An **abacus** is a frame with beads that move along pieces of wire. It is used for counting.

گنتارا

able
If you are **able** to do something, you know how to do it.

اہل، قابل

*She is **able** to swim.*

about
1 **About** means to do with.

بارے میں

*This book is **about** history.*

2 **About** also means near to something.

تقریباً، لگ بھگ

*His grandfather is **about** 80 years old.*

above

If something is **above** another thing, it is over it or higher than it.

اوپر

*Lift the ball **above** your head.*

accident *noun*
accidents

1 An **accident** is something nasty that happens, and that hurts someone.

حادثہ

*He broke his leg in a car **accident**.*

2 If something happens by **accident**, you do not expect it to happen.

غلطی سے

*I dropped a cup by **accident**.*

ache *verb*
aches, aching, ached

If a part of your body **aches**, you feel a steady pain there.

درد ہونا

*My leg **aches** a lot.*

acorn *noun*
acorns

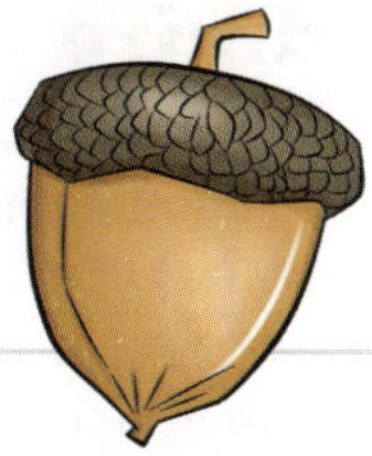

An **acorn** is the seed of an oak tree.

شاہ بلوط کا پھل

across
If someone goes **across** a place, they go from one side of it to the other.

آر پار

*She walked **across** the road.*

act *verb*
acts, acting, acted

1 When you **act**, you do something.

کارروائی کرنا

*The police **acted** quickly to stop the fight.*

2 If you **act** in a play or film, you pretend to be one of the people in it.

کردار ادا کرنا

active *adjective*
Someone who is **active** moves around a lot.

فعال

*My grandmother is very **active** for her age.*

add *verb*
adds, adding, added

1 If you **add** one thing to another, you put it with the other thing.

شامل کرنا، ملانا

***Add** the water to the flour.*

2 If you **add** numbers together, you find out how many they make together.

جوڑنا

***Add** three and six.*

address *noun*
addresses

Your **address** is the name of the place where you live.

پتہ

adjective *noun*
adjectives

An **adjective** is a word like "big" or "beautiful", that tells you more about a person or thing.

اسم صفت

A B C D E F G H I J K L M N O P Q R S T U V W X Y Z

admire *verb*
admires, admiring, admired

If you **admire** something, you like it and think that it is very nice or very good.

تعریف کرنا

*I **admired** his painting.*

adopt *verb*
adopts, adopting, adopted

If you **adopt** another person's child, you take them into your own family as your son or daughter.

گود لینا

adult *noun*
adults

An **adult** is a person who is not a child anymore.

بالغ

adventure *noun*
adventures

An **adventure** is something exciting which you do, or which happens to you.

مہم جوئی

*He wrote a book about his **adventures** in the jungle.*

adverb *noun*
adverbs

An **adverb** is a word like "slowly", "now", or "very" that tells you about how something is done.

متعلق فعل

aeroplane *noun*
aeroplanes

An **aeroplane** is a large vehicle with wings and engines that flies through the air.

ہوائی جہاز، طیارہ

afraid *adjective*

If you are **afraid**, you are frightened because you think that something bad will happen to you.

ڈرا ہوا

*I am not **afraid** of the dark.*

after

1 If something happens **after** another thing, it happens later than it.

بعد

*I watched television **after** dinner.*

2 If you go **after** a person or thing, you follow them or chase them.

پیچھے

*They ran **after** her.*

afternoon *noun*
afternoons

The **afternoon** is the part of each day between twelve noon and about six o'clock.

سہ پہر

again

If something happens **again**, it happens another time.

دوبارہ

*We went to the park **again** yesterday.*

against

1 If something is **against** another thing, it is touching it.

کے سہارے

*He leaned **against** the wall.*

2 If you play **against** someone in a game, you try to beat them.

خلاف

*The two teams played **against** one another.*

age *noun*
ages

Your **age** is the number of years that you have lived.

عمر

ago

You use **ago** to talk about a time in the past.

قبل، پہلے

*She left two weeks **ago**.*

agree *verb*
agrees, agreeing, agreed
If you **agree** with someone, you think the same as they do about something.
راضی ہونا
*I **agree** with you about him.*

ahead
Someone who is **ahead** of another person is in front of them.
آگے
*My brother ran **ahead** of us.*

air *noun*
Air is the mixture of gases all around us that we breathe.
ہوا
*I opened the window and let in some **air**.*

aircraft *noun*
aircraft
An **aircraft** is any vehicle which can fly.
طیارہ

airport *noun*
airports
An **airport** is a place where aeroplanes fly from and land.
ہوائی اڈہ

alarm *noun*
alarms
An **alarm** is a piece of equipment that warns you of danger by making a noise.
الارم
*The car **alarm** woke us up.*

alien *noun*
aliens
In stories and films, an **alien** is a creature from another planet.
خلائی مخلوق

alike *adjective*
If people or things are **alike**, they are the same in some way.
ایک جیسا، یکساں
*The two cats looked **alike**.*

alive *adjective*
If a person, an animal or a plant is **alive**, they are living and not dead.
زندہ

all
You use **all** to talk about everything, everyone, or the whole of something.
سبھی، تمام
*Did you eat **all** of it?*

alligator *noun*
alligators
An **alligator** is a large reptile with a long body, a long mouth and sharp teeth. **Alligators'** mouths are in the shape of a letter U.
گھڑیال

allow *verb*
allows, allowing, allowed
If you **allow** someone to do something, you let them do it.
اجازت دینا
*Mum **allowed** us to go out and play.*

A B C D E F G H I J K L M N O P Q R S T U V W X Y Z

all right or alright *adjective*

If you say that something is **all right**, you mean that it is good enough.

اچھا، اچھی، ٹھیک

*I thought the film was **all right**.*

almost

Almost means very nearly.

زیادہ تر

*I **almost** missed the bus.*

alone *adjective*

When you are **alone**, you are not with any other people.

تنہا

*She was **alone** in the room.*

along

1 If you walk **along** a road or other place, you move towards one end of it.

کے ساتھ، پر

*We walked **along** the street.*

2 If you bring something **along** when you go somewhere, you bring it with you.

ساتھ

*She brought a present **along** to the party.*

aloud

When you read or talk **aloud**, you read or talk so that other people can hear you.

زور سے

*She read the story **aloud** to us.*

alphabet *noun*

alphabets

An **alphabet** is a set of letters that is used for writing words. The letters are arranged in a special order.

حروف تہجی

*A is the first letter of the **alphabet**.*

already

You use **already** to show that something has happened before the present time.

پہلے سے

*She is **already** here.*

also

You use **also** to give more information about something.

بھی

*I'm cold, and I'm **also** hungry.*

always

If you **always** do something, you do it every time or all the time.

ہمیشہ

*She's **always** late for school.*

am

⇨ Look at **be**.

*I **am** six years old.*

amazing *adjective*

You say that something is **amazing** when it is a surprise and you like it.

حیرت انگیز

*We had an **amazing** holiday.*

ambulance *noun*

ambulances

An **ambulance** is a vehicle for taking people to hospital.

ایمبولنس

amount *noun*

amounts

An **amount** of something is how much there is of it.

مقدار

*We only have a small **amount** of food.*

amphibian *noun*

amphibians

An **amphibian** is an animal that lives both on land and in water, for example a frog or a toad.

بر بحری جانور

ancient *adjective*

Ancient means very old, or from a long time ago.

قدیم

*They lived in an **ancient** castle.*

angry *adjective*

angrier, angriest

When you are **angry**, you feel very upset about something.

ناراض

*She was **angry** at her brother for breaking the window.*

animal *noun*

animals

An **animal** is any creature that is alive, but not a plant or a person.

جانور

ankle *noun*

ankles

Your **ankle** is the part of your body where your foot joins your leg.

ٹخنہ

*I fell and twisted my **ankle**.*

annoy *verb*

annoys, annoying, annoyed

If something **annoys** you, it makes you angry and upset.

غصہ دلانا

*It **annoys** me when people are rude.*

another

You use **another** to mean one more.

ایک دوسرا

*She ate **another** cake.*

answer *verb*

answers, answering, answered

If you **answer** someone, you say something back to them.

جواب دینا

*She said hello, but he didn't **answer**.*

ant *noun*

ants

Ants are small insects that live in large groups.

چیونٹی

antelope *noun*

antelopes

An **antelope** is an animal that looks like a deer.

بارہ سنگھا

any

1 You use **any** to mean some of a thing.

کچھ

*Is there **any** juice left?*

2 You also use **any** to show that it does not matter which one.

کوئی

*Take **any** book you want.*

anybody

You use **anybody** to talk about a person, when it does not matter which one.

کوئی شخص

*Is there **anybody** there?*

anyone

You use **anyone** to talk about a person, when it does not matter who.

کوئی بھی

*Don't tell **anyone**.*

anything

You use **anything** to talk about a thing, when it does not matter which one.

کوئی چیز

*I can't see **anything**.*

A B C D E F G H I J K L M N O P Q R S T U V W X Y Z

anywhere

You use **anywhere** to talk about a place, when it does not matter which one.

کہیں بھی

*You can go **anywhere** you like.*

apart

1 When things are **apart**, there is a space or a distance between them.

الگ

*The desks are too far **apart**.*

2 If you take something **apart**, you take it to pieces.

الگ کرنا

*He took his bike **apart**.*

ape *noun*

apes

An **ape** is an animal like a large monkey with long, strong arms and no tail.

بن مانس، بوزنہ

apologize

or **apologise** *verb*

apologizes, apologizing, apologized

When you **apologize**, you say that you are sorry for something you have said or done.

معافی مانگنا

*He **apologized** for breaking the window.*

appear *verb*

appears, appearing, appeared

When something **appears**, it becomes possible to see it.

ظاہر ہونا

*The sun **appeared** from behind the clouds.*

apple *noun*

apples

An **apple** is a firm, round fruit with green, red, or yellow skin.

سیب

April *noun*

April is the month after March and before May. It has 30 days.

اپریل

*His birthday is in **April**.*

apron *noun*

aprons

An **apron** is a large piece of cloth that you wear over your other clothes to keep them clean when you are cooking or painting.

لبادہ

are

⇨ Look at **be**.

*They **are** both in my class.*

area *noun*

areas

An **area** is a part of a place.

علاقہ

*We live in an **area** near the park.*

aren't

Aren't is short for **are not**.

*My friends **aren't** here today.*

argue *verb*

argues, arguing, argued

If you **argue** with someone, you talk about something that you do not agree about.

بحث کرنا

*We **argued** about where to go.*

argument *noun*

arguments

If you have an **argument** with someone, you talk about something that you do not agree about.

دلیل

*She had an **argument** with another girl.*

arm *noun*

arms

Your **arms** are the two parts of your body between your shoulders and your hands.

بازو

*She stretched her **arms** out.*

armchair *noun*

armchairs

An **armchair** is a big comfortable chair with parts on the sides for you to put your arms on.

آرام کرسی

army *noun*

armies

An **army** is a large group of soldiers who fight in a war.

فوج

around

1 **Around** means in a circle.

چاروں طرف

*There were lots of people **around** her.*

2 You also use **around** to say that something is in every part of a place.

اردگرد

*His toys lay **around** the room.*

3 **Around** also means near to something.

آس پاس، قریب

*We left **around** noon.*

arrange *verb*

arranges, arranging, arranged

1 If you **arrange** something, you make plans for it to happen.

انتظام کرنا

*We **arranged** a party for her birthday.*

2 If you **arrange** things somewhere, you put them in a way that looks tidy or pretty.

ترتیب دینا

*He **arranged** the books in piles.*

arrive *verb*

arrives, arriving, arrived

When you **arrive** at a place, you get there.

آنا

*We **arrived** ten minutes late.*

arrow *noun*

arrows

1 An **arrow** is a long, thin stick with a sharp point at one end.

تیر

*The soldiers used bows and **arrows**.*

2 An **arrow** is also a sign that shows you which way to go.

تیر کا نشان

*Follow the **arrows** along the path.*

art *noun*

Art is something that someone has made for people to look at, for example a painting or drawing.

فنون لطیفہ

ask *verb*

asks, asking, asked

1 If you **ask** someone a question, you say that you want to know something.

پوچھنا

*I **asked** him what his name was.*

2 If you **ask** for something, you say that you want it.

طلب کرنا

*She **asked** for some sweets.*

asleep *adjective*

If you are **asleep**, you are sleeping.

خوابیدہ

*The cat was **asleep** under the tree.*

assembly *noun*

assemblies

An **assembly** is a group of people who meet together.

اسمبلی، اجتماع

*We were late for school **assembly**.*

assistant *noun*

assistants

An **assistant** is someone who helps another person in their work.

معاون

astronaut *noun*

astronauts

An **astronaut** is a person who travels in space.

خلا باز

a b c d e f g h i j k l m n o p q r s t u v w x y z

ate

⇨ Look at **eat**.

*He **ate** three apples.*

atlas *noun*

atlases

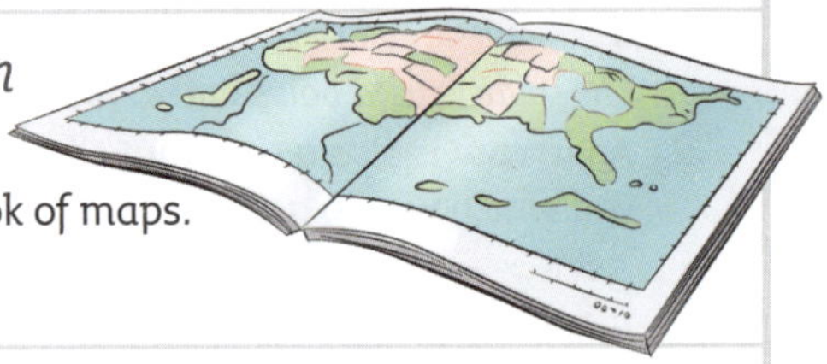

An **atlas** is a book of maps.

ایٹلس، خریطہ

attack *verb*

attacks, attacking, attacked

If someone **attacks** another person, they try to hurt them.

حملہ کرنا

attention *noun*

If you pay **attention**, you watch and listen.

توجہ

*He always pays **attention** in class.*

attract *verb*

attracts, attracting, attracted

If something **attracts** things to it, it makes them move towards it.

راغب کرنا

*Magnets **attract** anything made of iron.*

audience *noun*

audiences

An **audience** is all of the people who watch or listen to something, for example a film or a play.

سامعین، ناظرین

August *noun*

August is the month after July and before September. It has 31 days.

اگست

*We went on holiday in **August**.*

aunt *noun*

aunts

Your **aunt** is the sister of your mother or father, or the wife of your uncle.

چچی، پھوپھی، ممانی، خالہ

author *noun*

authors

An **author** is a person who writes books.

مصنف

autumn *noun*

autumns

Autumn is the season after summer and before winter. In the **autumn** the weather usually becomes cooler and the leaves fall off the trees.

خزاں

awake *adjective*

Someone who is **awake** is not sleeping.

جاگنا

*I stayed **awake** until midnight.*

away

1. If someone moves **away** from a place, they move so that they are not there any more.

   دور

   *He walked **away** from the house.*

2. If you put something **away**, you put it where it should be.

   جگہ پر رکھنا

   *Put your books **away** before you go.*

awful *adjective*

If something is **awful**, it is very bad.

ناگوار

*There was an **awful** smell.*

axe *noun*

axes

An **axe** is a tool with a handle and a big, sharp blade. It is used to chop wood.

کلہاڑی

Bb

baby *noun*
babies
A **baby** is a very young child.
بچہ

back *noun*
backs
1 Your **back** is the part of your body from your neck to your bottom.
پیٹھ
*He was lying on his **back** in the grass.*
2 The **back** of something is the side or part of it that is farthest from the front.
پیچھے
*She was in a room at the **back** of the shop.*

backwards
1 If you move **backwards**, you move in the direction behind you.
پیچھے کی طرف
*She walked **backwards**.*
2 If you do something **backwards**, you do it the opposite of the usual way.
الٹی طرف
*He had his jumper on **backwards**.*

bad *adjective*
worse, worst
1 Something that is **bad** is not nice or good.
خراب
*The weather is **bad** today.*
2 Someone who is **bad** does things they should not do.
خراب، بدمعاش
*Some **bad** boys stole the money.*

badge *noun*
badges
A **badge** is a small piece of metal or plastic with words or a picture on it that you wear on your clothes.
بلا

badger *noun*
badgers
A **badger** is an animal that has a white head with two black stripes on it. **Badgers** live beneath the ground and come out at night.
بجو

bag *noun*
bags
A **bag** is a container that you use to hold or carry things.
تھیلا
*He put his shoes in his **bag**.*

bake *verb*
bakes, baking, baked
When you **bake** food, you cook it in an oven.
سینکنا

baker *noun*
bakers
A **baker** is a person who makes and sells bread and cakes.
بیکری والا

balance *verb*
balances, balancing, balanced
When you **balance** something, you keep it steady and do not let it fall.
توازن
*She **balanced** a book on her head.*

ball *noun*
balls
A **ball** is a round thing that you kick, throw or catch in games.
گیند

ballet *noun*
Ballet is a kind of dance with special steps that often tells a story.
بیلے

A B C D E F G H I J K L M N O P Q R S T U V W X Y Z

balloon *noun*
balloons
A **balloon** is a small bag made of thin rubber that you blow into to make it bigger.
غبارہ

banana *noun*
bananas
A **banana** is a long curved fruit with a thick yellow skin.
کیلا

band *noun*
bands
1 A **band** is a group of people who play music together.
بینڈ، سازندہ جماعت
*He plays the guitar in a **band**.*
2 A **band** is also a narrow strip of material that you put around something.
رکاوٹ
*She wore a **band** round her hair.*

bandage *noun*
bandages
A **bandage** is a long strip of cloth that you wrap around a part of your body when you have hurt it.
پٹی

bang *noun*
bangs
A **bang** is a sudden, loud noise.
دھماکہ
*The balloon burst with a **bang**.*

bank *noun*
banks
1 A **bank** is a place where people can keep their money.
بینک
*He got some money from the **bank**.*
2 A **bank** is also the ground beside a river.
کنارہ
*We walked along the **bank**.*

bar *noun*
bars
A **bar** is a long, thin piece of wood or metal.
چھڑ
*There were **bars** on the windows.*

bare *adjective*
barer, barest
1 If a part of your body is **bare**, it is not covered by any clothes.
ننگا
*Her feet were **bare**.*
2 If something is **bare**, it has nothing on top of it or inside it.
کھلا
*The cupboard was **bare**.*

bark *verb*
barks, barking, barked
When a dog **barks**, it makes a short, loud noise.
بھونکنا

barn *noun*
barns
A **barn** is a big building on a farm where animals and crops are kept.
کھلیان

base *noun*
bases
The **base** of something is the lowest part of it, or the part that it stands on.
اساس
*She stood at the **base** of the stairs.*

basket *noun*
baskets
A **basket** is a container that you use to hold or carry things. It is made from thin strips of material.
ٹوکری

bat *noun*
bats
1 A **bat** is a special stick that you use to hit a ball in some games.
بلا
2 A **bat** is also a small animal that looks like a mouse with wings. **Bats** come out to fly at night.
چمگادڑ

bath *noun*
baths
A **bath** is a long container that you fill with water and sit in to wash yourself.
غسل ٹب

bathroom *noun*
bathrooms
A **bathroom** is a room with a bath or shower in it.
غسل خانہ

battery *noun*
batteries
A **battery** is a small tube or box for storing electricity. You put **batteries** in things like toys and radios to make them work.
بیٹری
The clock needs a new ***battery****.*

be *verb*
am, is, are, being, was, were, been
1 You use **be** to say what a person or thing is like.
ہونا
She ***is*** *very young.*
2 You also use **be** to say that something is there.
موجود ہونا
There ***is*** *a tree in the garden.*

beach *noun*
beaches
A **beach** is the land by the edge of the sea. It is covered with sand or stones.
ساحل

bead *noun*
beads
A **bead** is a small piece of glass, wood or plastic with a hole through the middle. You put **beads** on a string to make necklaces or bracelets.
منکا

beak *noun*
beaks
A bird's **beak** is the hard part of its mouth.
چونچ

bean *noun*
beans
A **bean** is the small seed of some plants that you can eat as a vegetable.
دانے

bear *noun*
bears
A **bear** is a big, strong animal with thick fur and sharp claws.
بھالو

beard *noun*
beards
A **beard** is the hair that grows on a man's chin and cheeks.
داڑھی

beat *verb*
beats, beating, beat, beaten
1 If you **beat** something, you keep hitting it.
مارنا
He ***beat*** *the drum with a stick.*
2 If you **beat** someone in a game or a competition, you do better than they do.
شکست دینا، ہرانا
He ***beat*** *me in the race.*

beautiful *adjective*
If something is **beautiful**, it is very nice to look at or to listen to.
خوبصورت
He painted a ***beautiful*** *picture.*

became
⇨ Look at **become**.
She ***became*** *very angry.*

because

You use **because** to say why something happens.

کیوں کہ

*I went to bed **because** I was tired.*

become *verb*

becomes, becoming, became, become

If one thing **becomes** another thing, it starts to be that thing.

ہونا

*The weather **became** cold.*

bed *noun*

beds

A **bed** is a piece of furniture that you lie on when you sleep.

بستر

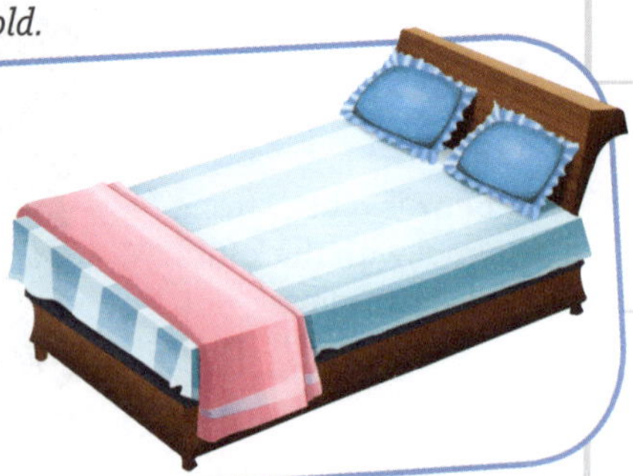

bedroom *noun*

bedrooms

A **bedroom** is a room with a bed in it where you sleep.

خواب گاہ

bedtime *noun*

bedtimes

Your **bedtime** is the time when you usually go to bed.

سونے کا وقت

*My **bedtime** is at eight o'clock.*

bee *noun*

bees

A **bee** is an insect with wings and black and yellow stripes on its body. **Bees** live in large groups and make honey.

شہد کی مکھی

been

⇨ Look at **be**.

*We have always **been** good friends.*

beetle *noun*

beetles

A **beetle** is an insect with hard wings that cover its body when it is not flying.

بھونرا

before

If one thing happens **before** another thing, it happens earlier than it.

قبل، پہلے

*My birthday is just **before** his.*

began

⇨ Look at **begin**.

*She **began** to laugh.*

begin *verb*

begins, beginning, began, begun

If you **begin** to do something, you start to do it.

شروع کرنا

*You can **begin** to write now.*

begun

⇨ Look at **begin**.

*He has **begun** to play the piano.*

behave *verb*

behaves, behaving, behaved

1 The way you **behave** is the way that you do and say things.

سلوک کرنا

*She **behaves** like a baby.*

2 If you **behave** yourself, you are good.

تمیز سے پیش آنا

*You can come if you **behave** yourself.*

behind

If something is **behind** another thing, it is at the back of it.

پیچھے

*He stood **behind** his desk.*

believe *verb*
believes, believing, believed
If you **believe** something, you think that it is true.
یقین کرنا
*I don't **believe** that story.*

bell *noun*
bells
A **bell** is a piece of metal in the shape of a cup that rings when you shake it or hit it.
گھنٹی

belong *verb*
belongs, belonging, belonged
1 If something **belongs** to you, it is yours.
متعلق ہونا، کا ہونا، وابستہ ہونا
*The book **belongs** to her.*
2 If you **belong** to a group of people, you are one of them.
وابستہ ہونا، متعلق ہونا، کا ہونا
*He **belongs** to our team.*
3 If something **belongs** somewhere, that is where it should be.
پر ہونا، اس جگہ پر ہونا
*Your toys **belong** in your room.*

below
If something is **below** another thing, it is lower down than it.
نیچے
*His shoes were **below** his bed.*

belt *noun*
belts
A **belt** is a band of leather or cloth that you wear around your waist.
پٹی

bench *noun*
benches
A **bench** is a long seat that two or more people can sit on.
بینچ

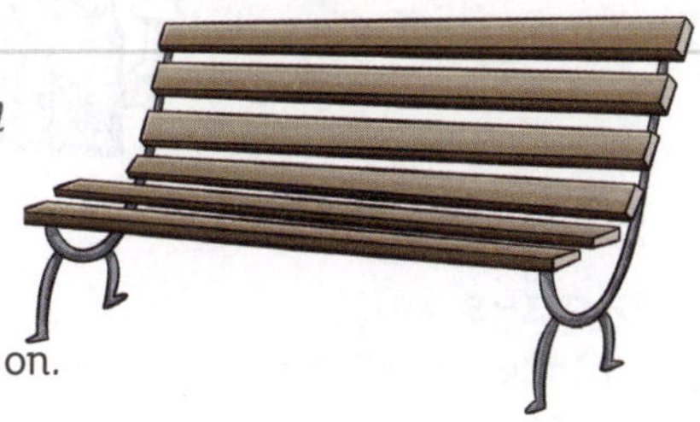

bend *verb*
bends, bending, bent
When you **bend** something, you change its shape so that it is not straight any more.
موڑنا
***Bend** your legs when you do this exercise.*

beneath
If something is **beneath** another thing, it is below it.
نیچے
*The dog was **beneath** the table.*

bent
⇨ Look at **bend**.
*He **bent** to pick up the bags.*

berry *noun*
berries
A **berry** is a small, soft fruit that grows on a bush or a tree.
بیر

beside
If something is **beside** another thing, it is next to it.
علاوہ
*He sat down **beside** me.*

best
If you say that something is **best**, you mean that it is better than all the others.
بہترین
*You are my **best** friend.*

A B C D E F G H I J K L M N O P Q R S T U V W X Y Z

better

1 You use **better** to mean that a thing is very good compared to another thing.

بہتر

*His painting is **better** than mine.*

2 If you feel **better**, you do not feel ill any more.

اچھا، صحت مند

*I feel much **better** today.*

between

If you are **between** two things, one of them is on one side of you and the other is on the other side.

درمیان

*She stood **between** her two brothers.*

bicycle *noun*

bicycles

A **bicycle** is a vehicle with two wheels. You push the pedals with your feet to make the wheels turn.

سائیکل

big *adjective*

bigger, biggest

A person or thing that is **big** is large in size.

بڑی

*She lives in a **big** house.*

bike *noun*

bikes

A **bike** is a bicycle or motorbike.

سائیکل، موٹر سائیکل

bin *noun*

bins

A **bin** is a container that you put rubbish in.

کوڑے دان

bird *noun*

birds

A **bird** is an animal with feathers, wings, and a beak. Most **birds** can fly.

پرندہ، چڑیا

birthday *noun*

birthdays

Your **birthday** is the date that you were born.

یومِ پیدائش

*She gave me a present on my **birthday**.*

biscuit *noun*

biscuits

A **biscuit** is a kind of small, hard, dry cake.

بسکٹ

bit *noun*

bits

A **bit** of something is a small amount of it, or a small part of it.

ٹکڑا

*I ate a **bit** of bread.*

bite *verb*

bites, biting, bit, bitten

If you **bite** something, you use your teeth to cut into it.

کاٹنا

*The dog tried to **bite** him.*

black *noun*

Black is the colour of the sky at night.

کالا

*The car is **black**.*

blackboard *noun*

blackboards

A **blackboard** is a flat, black surface that you write on with chalk in a classroom.

تختۂ سیاہ

blade *noun*

blades

A **blade** is the flat, sharp part of a knife that you use to cut things.

دھار

blame *verb*

blames, blaming, blamed

If you **blame** someone for something bad, you think that they made it happen.

الزام دینا

*Mum **blamed** me for making the mess.*

blanket *noun*

blankets

A **blanket** is a large, thick piece of cloth that you put on a bed to keep you warm.

کمبل

blew

➪ Look at **blow**.

*The wind **blew** outside.*

blind *adjective*

Someone who is **blind** cannot see.

اندھا

block *noun*

blocks

A **block** of something is a large piece of it with straight sides.

بلاک، مربع نما ٹکڑا

*We made a house with **blocks** of wood.*

blood *noun*

Blood is the red liquid that moves around inside your body.

خون

blouse *noun*

blouses

A **blouse** is something a girl or woman can wear. It covers the top part of the body and has buttons down the front.

بلاوز

blow *verb*

blows, blowing, blew, blown

1 When the wind **blows**, it moves the air.

بہنا

2 When you **blow**, you push air out of your mouth.

پھونک مارنا

*He **blew** on his hands to keep them warm.*

blue *noun*

Blue is the colour of the sky on a sunny day.

نیلا

*Her dress is **blue**.*

blunt *adjective*

blunter, bluntest

Something that is **blunt** does not have a sharp point or edge.

کند ہونا

*My pencil is **blunt**.*

boat *noun*

boats

A **boat** is a small vehicle that carries people on water.

ناو

body *noun*

bodies

A person's or animal's **body** is all their parts.

جسم

*It's fun to stretch and twist your **body**.*

boil *verb*

boils, boiling, boiled

1 When water **boils**, it becomes very hot, and you can see bubbles in it and steam coming from it.

ابلنا، کافی گرم ہونا

2 When you **boil** food, you cook it in water that is boiling.

ابالنا

bone *noun*

bones

Your **bones** are the hard parts inside your body.

ہڈی

*I broke a **bone** in my leg.*

bonfire *noun*
bonfires
A **bonfire** is a big fire that is made outside.
آگ

book *noun*
books
A **book** is a set of pages with words or pictures on them, that are held together inside a cover.
کتاب

boot *noun*
boots
A **boot** is a kind of shoe that covers your foot and the lower part of your leg.
بوٹ (جوتے)

bored *adjective*
If you are **bored**, you feel annoyed because you have nothing to do.
بے زار

boring *adjective*
If something is **boring**, it is not interesting.
بے زار کن

born *verb*
When a baby is **born**, it comes out of its mother's body.
پیدا ہونا
*My sister was **born** three years ago.*

borrow *verb*
borrows, borrowing, borrowed
If you **borrow** something from someone, they let you have it for a short time and then you give it back.
ادھار لینا
*Can I **borrow** your pen, please?*

both
You use **both** to mean two people or two things together.
دونوں
*He put **both** books into the drawer.*

bottle *noun*
bottles
A **bottle** is a container made of glass or plastic that holds liquid.
بوتل

bottom *noun*
bottoms
1 The **bottom** of something is its lowest part.
نچلا حصہ، پیندا
2 Your **bottom** is the part of your body that you sit on.
چوتڑ، سرین

bought
⇨ Look at **buy**.
*We **bought** bread and milk.*

bounce *verb*
bounces, bouncing, bounced
When something **bounces**, it hits another thing and then moves away from it again.
اچھلنا
*The ball **bounced** across the floor.*

bow *verb*
bows, bowing, bowed
When you **bow**, you bend your body towards someone as a polite way of saying hello or thanking them.
جھکنا
*They all **bowed** to the king.*

bow *noun*
bows
1 A **bow** is a knot with two loose ends that you use to tie laces and ribbons.
بو، ٹائی
2 A **bow** is also a long, curved piece of wood with a string stretched between the two ends, that is used to send arrows through the air.
کمان

bowl *noun*
bowls
A **bowl** is a round container that you use to hold food or drink.
بڑا پیالا

box *noun*
boxes
A **box** is a container with a hard, straight bottom and sides, and usually a lid.
بکس

boy *noun*
boys
A **boy** is a male child.
لڑکا

bracelet *noun*
bracelets
A **bracelet** is a chain or a band that you wear around your wrist.
بازوبند

brain *noun*
brains
Your **brain** is inside your head. It controls your body and lets you think and feel things.
مغز

branch *noun*
branches
The **branches** of a tree are the parts that grow out from its trunk and have leaves on them.
شاخ

brave *adjective*
braver, bravest
If you are **brave**, you are not afraid of something dangerous.
بہادر

bread *noun*
Bread is a food that is made from flour and water and baked in an oven.
روٹی

break *verb*
breaks, breaking, broke, broken
1 When something **breaks**, it goes into pieces.
ٹوٹنا
I dropped a plate and it ***broke****.*
2 When a machine **breaks**, it stops working.
رک جانا، کام کرنا بند کر دینا
My brother ***broke*** *the television.*

breakfast *noun*
breakfasts
Breakfast is the first meal of the day.
ناشتہ

breathe *verb*
breathes, breathing, breathed
When you **breathe**, air goes in and out of your body through your nose or your mouth.
سانس لینا

brick *noun*
bricks
Bricks are small blocks of baked earth used for building.
اینٹ

bride *noun*
brides
A **bride** is a woman who is getting married.
دلہن

A B C D E F G H I J K L M N O P Q R S T U V W X Y Z

bridegroom *noun*
bridegrooms
A **bridegroom** is a man who is getting married.
دولہا

bridge *noun*
bridges
A **bridge** is something that is built over a river, a road, or a railway so that people can get across it.
پل

bright *adjective*
brighter, brightest
1 A **bright** colour is very easy to see.
چمکیلا، بھڑکیلا
*She wore a **bright** red dress.*
2 Something that is **bright** shines with a lot of light.
چمکدار
*The sun is very **bright** today.*

brilliant *adjective*
Something that is **brilliant** is very good.
بہترین، ذہانت سے بھرپور
*I thought the film was **brilliant**.*

bring *verb*
brings, bringing, brought
If you **bring** something, you take it with you when you go somewhere.
لانا
*You can **bring** a friend to the party.*

broke
⇨ Look at **break**.
*I'm sorry I **broke** the radio.*

broken *adjective*
If something is **broken**, it is in pieces.
ٹوٹا ہوا
*All of his toys are **broken**.*

broom *noun*
brooms
A **broom** is a brush with a long handle that you use to sweep the floor.
جھاڑو

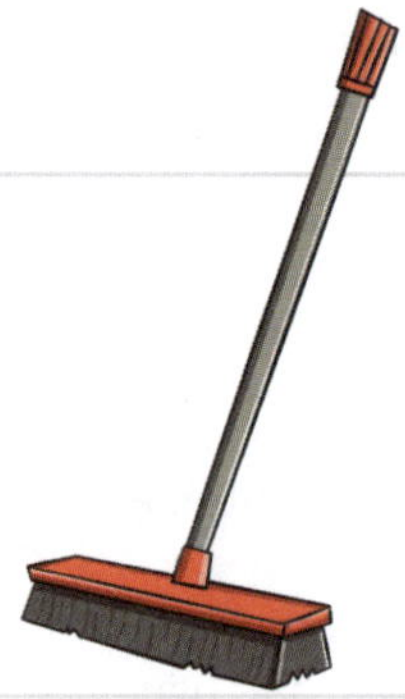

brother *noun*
brothers
Your **brother** is a boy or a man who has the same mother and father as you do.
بھائی

brought
⇨ Look at **bring**.
*We **brought** some food for the picnic.*

brown *noun*
Brown is the colour of earth or wood.
بھورا
*Her eyes are dark **brown**.*

bruise *noun*
bruises
A **bruise** is a purple mark on your skin that appears if something hits a part of your body.
خراش
*She has a big **bruise** on her leg.*

brush *noun*
brushes
A **brush** has lots of short hairs fixed to a handle. You use a **brush** to make your hair tidy, to clean things, or to paint.
برش

bubble *noun*
bubbles
A **bubble** is a small ball of liquid with air inside it.
بلبلہ

bucket *noun*

buckets
A **bucket** is a deep, round container with a handle that you use to hold or carry liquids.
بالٹی

buckle *noun*

buckles
A **buckle** is something you use to fasten a belt, a shoe or a bag.
بکل

bud *noun*
buds
A **bud** is a small, new part on a tree or plant that grows into a leaf or a flower.
کلی

build *verb*
builds, building, built
If you **build** something, you make it by putting the parts of it together.
بنانا
*They are going to **build** the school here.*

building *noun*
buildings
A **building** is a place with walls and a roof.
عمارت سازی
*Houses, shops and schools are all **buildings**.*

built
⇨ Look at **build**.
*We **built** our house on a hill.*

bulb *noun*

bulbs
A **bulb** is the part of a lamp that is made of glass and gives out light.
بلب

bull *noun*
bulls
A **bull** is a male cow. **Bulls** have horns.
سانڈ

bump *verb*
bumps, bumping, bumped
If you **bump** something, or **bump** into it, you hit it without meaning to.
حادثاتی ٹکراو
*I **bumped** the table with my bag.*

bunch *noun*
bunches
A **bunch** of things is a group of them.
گچھا
*He held a **bunch** of keys.*

bundle *noun*

bundles
A **bundle** is a lot of clothes, sticks or other things that are fastened together.
گٹھری

buried
⇨ Look at **bury**.
*The pirates **buried** the gold beneath a tree.*

burn *verb*
burns, burning, burned, burnt
1 If you **burn** something, you destroy it or damage it with fire.
جلانا
*He **burned** all the rubbish.*
2 If you **burn** yourself, you touch something that is hot and get hurt.
جلانا
*I **burned** myself on the hot iron.*
3 If something is **burning**, it is on fire.
جلنا
*The bonfire is still **burning**.*

burst *verb*
bursts, bursting, burst
When something **bursts**, it breaks open suddenly.
پھٹنا
*The bag **burst** and everything fell out of it.*

bury *verb*
buries, burying, buried
If you **bury** something, you put it into a hole in the ground and cover it up.
دفنانا
*Squirrels **bury** nuts to eat in the winter.*

bus *noun*
buses
A **bus** is a large vehicle that carries lots of people.
بس
*I go to school on the **bus**.*

bush *noun*
bushes
A **bush** is a plant with lots of leaves and branches that is smaller than a tree.
جھاڑی

busy *adjective*
busier, busiest
1 If you are **busy**, you have a lot of things to do.
مصروف
*We were **busy** cleaning the house.*
2 A **busy** place is full of people.
بھیڑ بھرا، مصروف
*The shops are **busy** today.*

butcher *noun*
butchers
A **butcher** is a person who sells meat.
قصاب

butter *noun*
Butter is a soft yellow and white food that is made from cream. You spread it on bread or cook with it.
مکھن

butterfly *noun*
butterflies
A **butterfly** is an insect with four large wings.
تتلی

button *noun*
buttons
Buttons are small, round things on clothes that you push through holes to fasten the clothes together.
بٹن

buy *verb*
buys, buying, bought
If you **buy** something, you pay money so that you can have it.
خریدنا
*We went into the shop to **buy** sweets.*

buzz *verb*
buzzes, buzzing, buzzed
If something **buzzes**, it makes a sound like a bee makes when it flies.
بھنبھناہٹ ہونا
*An insect **buzzed** around my head.*

Cc

cabbage *noun*
cabbages
A **cabbage** is a round vegetable with green, white, or purple leaves.
بند گوبھی

cage *noun*
cages
A **cage** is a box or a room made of bars where you keep birds or animals.
پنجرہ

cake *noun*
cakes
A **cake** is a sweet food made from flour, eggs, sugar, and butter that you bake in an oven.
کیک

calculator *noun*
calculators
A **calculator** is a small machine that you use to do sums.
کیلکولیٹر

calendar *noun*
calendars
A **calendar** is a list of all the days, weeks, and months in a year.
کلینڈر

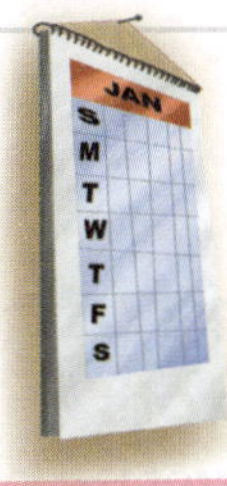

calf *noun*
calves
1 A **calf** is a young cow.
بچھڑا
2 Your **calves** are also the thick parts at the backs of your legs, between your ankles and your knees.
پنڈلی

call *verb*
calls, calling, called
1 If you **call** someone something, you give them a name.
پکارنا، نام دینا
*I **called** my cat Pippin.*
2 If you **call** something, you say it in a loud voice.
پکارنا
*Someone **called** his name.*
3 If you **call** someone, you talk to them on the telephone.
فون کرنا، کال کرنا
*I'll **call** you tomorrow.*

calves
⇨ Look at **calf**.
*My **calves** hurt.*

came
⇨ Look at **come**.
*My friends **came** to play at my house.*

camel *noun*
camels
A **camel** is a large animal with one or two big lumps on its back. **Camels** live in hot, dry places and carry people and things.
اونٹ

camera *noun*
cameras
A **camera** is a machine that you use to take pictures.
کیمرا

camp *noun*
camps
A **camp** is a place where people live in tents for a short time.
کیمپ، خیمہ

can *verb*
could
If you **can** do something, you are able to do it.
سکنا، کرنے کے قابل ہونا
*I **can** swim.*

A B C D E F G H I J K L M N O P Q R S T U V W X Y Z

can *noun*
cans
A **can** is a metal container for food or drink.
ڈبہ، ٹن
*She opened a **can** of soup.*

candle *noun*
candles
A **candle** is a stick of wax with a piece of string through the middle that you burn to give you light.
موم بتی

cannot *verb*
If you **cannot** do something, you are not able to do it.
نہیں کر سکنا، کرنے کے قابل نہ ہونا
*I **cannot** find my bag.*

can't
Can't is short for **cannot**.
*He **can't** play the piano.*

capital *noun*
capitals
1 The **capital** of a country is the main city, where the country's leaders work.
دارالسلطنت، دارالحکومت، راجدھانی
*Paris is the **capital** of France.*
2 A **capital** is also a big letter of the alphabet, for example A or R.
انگریزی کا بڑا حروف

car *noun*
cars
A **car** is a vehicle with four wheels and an engine that can carry a small number of people.
کار

card *noun*
cards
1 **Card** is stiff paper.
کارڈ، موٹا سخت کاغذ
2 A **card** is a folded piece of stiff paper that has a picture on the front and a message inside. You send **cards** to people at special times, like birthdays.
کارڈ، تاش کے پتے
3 **Cards** are pieces of stiff paper with numbers or pictures on them that you use for playing games.
تاش

cardboard *noun*
Cardboard is very thick, stiff paper that is used for making boxes.
کارڈبورڈ

care *verb*
cares, caring, cared
1 If you **care** about something, you think that it is important.
خیال رکھنا
*He doesn't **care** about the way he looks.*
2 If you **care** for a person or an animal, you look after them.
دیکھ بھال کرنا، نگہداشت کرنا
*She **cared** for her pets.*

careful *adjective*
If you are **careful**, you think about what you are doing so that you do not make any mistakes.
محتاط
*Be **careful** when you cross the road.*

careless *adjective*
If you are **careless**, you do not think about what you are doing, so that you make mistakes.
لاپرواہ
*It was **careless** of me to forget my keys.*

carpet *noun*
carpets
A **carpet** is a thick, soft cover for a floor.
قالین

carrot *noun*
carrots
A **carrot** is a long, orange vegetable.
گاجر

carry *verb*
carries, carrying, carried
If you **carry** something, you hold it and take it somewhere with you.
لے جانا
*We **carried** our bags to the car.*

carton *noun*
cartons

A **carton** is a container made of plastic or cardboard that is used to hold food or drink.

کارٹن

*I bought a **carton** of milk.*

cartoon *noun*
cartoons

1 A **cartoon** is a funny drawing.
کارٹون

2 A **cartoon** is also a film that uses drawings, not real people or things.
کارٹون فلم

case *noun*
cases

A **case** is a container that is used to hold or carry something.

خول

*He put the camera in its **case**.*

castle *noun*
castles

A **castle** is a large building with very thick, high walls. Most **castles** were built a long time ago to keep the people inside safe from their enemies.

محل

cat *noun*
cats

A **cat** is an animal that is covered with fur and has a long tail. People often keep small **cats** as pets. Large **cats**, for example lions and tigers, are wild.

بلی

catch *verb*
catches, catching, caught

1 If you **catch** something that is moving, you take hold of it while it is in the air.
ہوا میں پکڑنا
*I tried to **catch** the ball.*

2 If you **catch** a bus or a train, you get on it.
پکڑنا
*We **caught** the bus to school.*

3 If you **catch** an illness, you become ill with it.
مبتلا ہونا
*He **caught** measles.*

caterpillar *noun*
caterpillars

A **caterpillar** is a small animal that looks like a worm with lots of short legs. **Caterpillars** turn into butterflies or moths.

لاروا

cattle *noun*

Cattle are cows and bulls.

مویشی

*There were **cattle** in the field.*

caught

⇨ Look at **catch**.

*I jumped and **caught** the ball.*

cauliflower *noun*
cauliflowers

A **cauliflower** is a big, round, white vegetable with green leaves.

پھول گوبھی

cave *noun*
caves

A **cave** is a big hole in the side of a hill or a mountain, or beneath the ground.

غار

CD *noun*
CDs

CD is short for compact disc.

سی ڈی

*I bought the band's new **CD**.*

a b c d e f g h i j k l m n o p q r s t u v w x y z

ceiling *noun*
ceilings
A **ceiling** is the part of a room that is above your head.
چھت

centimetre *noun*
centimetres
A **centimetre** is used for measuring the length of something. There are ten millimetres in a **centimetre**, and one hundred **centimetres** in a metre.
سینٹی میٹر

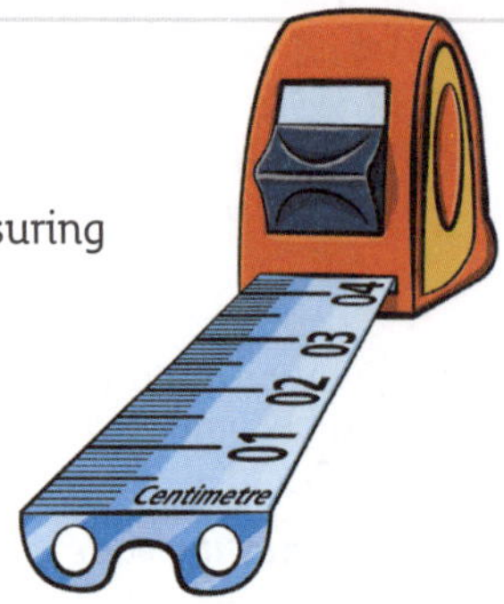

centre *noun*
centres
The **centre** of something is the middle of it.
مرکز
*She stood in the **centre** of the room.*

cereal *noun*
cereals
1 A **cereal** is a food made from grains that you eat with milk for breakfast.
اناج، سیریل
2 A **cereal** is also a kind of plant, for example wheat or rice. The seeds of **cereals** are used for food.
اناج کا پودا

chain *noun*
chains
A **chain** is a row of rings made of metal that are joined together in a line.
زنجیر

chair *noun*
chairs
A **chair** is a seat with a back and four legs, for one person.
کرسی
*He suddenly got up from his **chair**.*

chalk *noun*
Chalk is a kind of soft rock. You use small sticks of **chalk** to write or draw on a blackboard.
چاک، کھریا

change *verb*
changes, changing, changed
1 When you **change** something, or when it **changes**, it becomes different.
تبدیل کرنا
*The caterpillar **changed** into a butterfly.*
2 When you **change**, you put on different clothes.
لباس تبدیل کرنا
*He **changed** to go to the party.*

change *noun*
Change is the money that you get back when you pay too much for something.
تبادلہ، مبادلہ

chapter *noun*
chapters
A **chapter** is a part of a book.
باب
*This book has ten **chapters**.*

character *noun*
characters
1 Your **character** is the kind of person you are.
عادات و خصلت
2 A **character** is also a person in a story or a film.
کردار

charge *verb*
charges, charging, charged
If someone **charges** you an amount of money for something, they ask you to pay that amount for it.
وصول کرنا
*They **charged** us too much for our meal.*

chase *verb*
chases, chasing, chased
If you **chase** someone, you run after them and try to catch them.
پیچھا کرنا
*The dog **chased** the cat.*

cheap *adjective*
cheaper, cheapest
If something is **cheap**, you do not have to pay a lot of money for it.
سستی
*Milk is very **cheap** in this shop.*

check *verb*
checks, checking, checked
If you **check** something, you make sure that it is right.
جانچ کرنا
*The teacher **checked** my homework.*

cheek *noun*
cheeks
Your **cheeks** are the sides of your face below your eyes.
گال
*My **cheeks** were red.*

cheer *verb*
cheers, cheering, cheered
When people **cheer**, they shout to show that they like something.
شاباشی دینا، حمایت میں نعرے لگانا
*We all **cheered** when he won the race.*

cheerful *adjective*
Someone who is **cheerful** is happy.
خوش باش

cheese *noun*
Cheese is a solid food that is made from milk.
پنیر

cheetah *noun*
cheetahs
A **cheetah** is a big wild cat with yellow fur and black spots.
چیتا

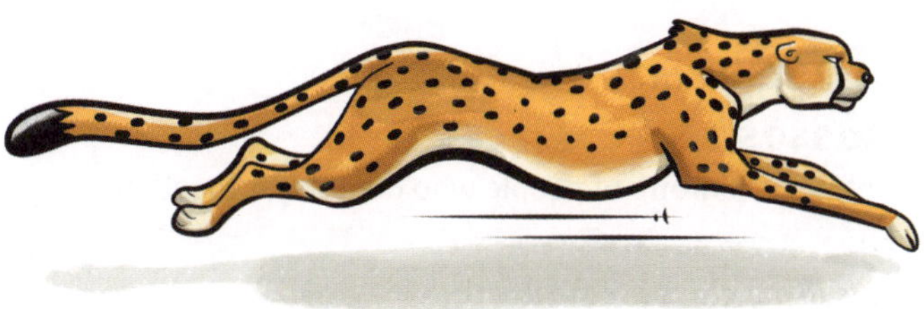

cherry *noun*
cherries
A **cherry** is a small, round fruit with a hard stone in the middle. **Cherries** are red, black, or yellow.
چیری

chew *verb*
chews, chewing, chewed
When you **chew** food, you use your teeth to break it up in your mouth before you swallow it.
چبانا

chick *noun*
chicks
A **chick** is a very young bird.
چوزہ

chicken *noun*
chickens
1 A **chicken** is a bird that is kept on a farm for its eggs and meat.
مرغ
2 **Chicken** is also the meat that comes from chickens.
مرغ کا گوشت

child *noun*
children
A **child** is a young boy or girl.
بچہ

chimney *noun*
chimneys
A **chimney** is a long pipe above a fire. Smoke from the fire goes up the **chimney** and out of the building.
چمنی

chimpanzee *noun*
chimpanzees
A **chimpanzee** is a kind of small ape with dark fur.
چمپینزی

chin *noun*
chins
Your **chin** is the part of your face below your mouth.
ٹھوڑی
A black beard covered his ***chin****.*

chip *noun*
chips
Chips or potato **chips** are thin pieces of potato fried in hot oil.
چپ، آلو کے پتلے تلے ہوئے قتلے

chip *verb*
chips, chipping, chipped
If you **chip** something, you break a small piece off it by accident.
توڑنا
I ***chipped*** *my tooth when I fell.*

chocolate *noun*
chocolates
Chocolate is a sweet brown food that is used to make sweets, cakes, and drinks.
چاکلیٹ

choose *verb*
chooses, choosing, chose, chosen
If you **choose** something, you decide to have it.
چننا
You can ***choose*** *any book you want.*

chop *verb*
chops, chopping, chopped
If you **chop** something, you cut it into pieces with a knife or an axe.
ٹکڑا
He ***chopped*** *some wood for the fire.*

chose
⇨ Look at **choose**.
She ***chose*** *a dress to wear.*

chosen
⇨ Look at **choose**.
We have ***chosen*** *which film to watch.*

circle *noun*
circles
A **circle** is a round shape.
دائرہ

circus *noun*
circuses
A **circus** is a big tent where you go to see clowns and animals.
سرکس

city *noun*
cities
A **city** is a very big town where a lot of people live and work.
شہر

clap *verb*
claps, clapping, clapped
When you **clap**, you hit your hands together to make a loud noise. People **clap** to show that they like something.
تالی بجانا
Everyone ***clapped*** *at the end of her song.*

class *noun*
classes
A **class** is a group of people who are taught together.
درجہ
He is in my ***class*** *at school.*

classroom *noun*
classrooms
A **classroom** is a room in a school where children have lessons.
کلاس روم

claw *noun*
claws
A bird's or an animal's **claws** are the hard, sharp, curved parts at the end of its feet.
پنجہ

clean *adjective*
cleaner, cleanest
Something that is **clean** does not have any dirt or marks on it.
صاف
*Make sure your hands are **clean**.*

clean *verb*
cleans, cleaning, cleaned
When you **clean** something, you take all the dirt off it.
صفائی کرنا
*I **clean** my teeth before bedtime.*

clear *adjective*
clearer, clearest

1. If something is **clear**, it is easy to understand, to see, or to hear.
   واضح
   *He gave us **clear** instructions on what to do.*
2. If something like glass or plastic is **clear**, you can see through it.
   شفاف
   *The bottle was full of a **clear** liquid.*
3. If a place is **clear**, it does not have anything there that you do not want.
   خالی ہونا
   *You can cross the road when it is **clear**.*

clear *verb*
clears, clearing, cleared
When you **clear** a place, you take away all the things you do not want there.
خالی کرنا
*She **cleared** the table.*

clever *adjective*
cleverer, cleverest
Someone who is **clever** can learn and understand things quickly.
چالاک
*She is very **clever** at maths.*

cliff *noun*
cliffs
A **cliff** is a hill with one side that is very steep. **Cliffs** are often beside the sea.
ٹیلا

climb *verb*
climbs, climbing, climbed
If you **climb** something, you move towards the top of it. You sometimes use your hands as well as your feet when you **climb**.
چڑھنا
*We **climbed** the tree in the garden.*

cloak *noun*
cloaks
A **cloak** is a very loose coat without sleeves.
چوغہ

clock *noun*
clocks
A **clock** is a machine that shows you the time.
گھڑی

close *verb*
closes, closing, closed
When you **close** something, you shut it.
بند کرنا
*Please **close** the door behind you.*

A B C D E F G H I J K L M N O P Q R S T U V W X Y Z

close *adjective*
closer, closest

If something is **close** to another thing, it is near it.

قریب ہونا

*Our house is **close** to the park.*

cloth *noun*
cloths

1 **Cloth** is material that is used to make things like clothes and curtains.

کپڑا

2 A **cloth** is a piece of material that you use to clean something.

صافی، پونچھا

clothes *noun*

Clothes are the things that people wear, for example shirts, trousers, and dresses.

کپڑے

cloud *noun*
clouds

A **cloud** is a white or grey shape that you see in the sky. **Clouds** are made of tiny drops of water that sometimes turn into rain.

بادل

clown *noun*
clowns

A **clown** is a person who wears funny clothes and does silly things to make people laugh.

مسخرہ

coat *noun*
coats

You wear a **coat** on top of your other clothes when you go outside.

کوٹ

cobweb *noun*
cobwebs

A **cobweb** is a very thin net that a spider makes to catch insects.

مکڑی کا جالہ

coconut *noun*
coconuts

A **coconut** is a very large nut that has a very hard shell and is white inside. **Coconuts** are full of a liquid called **coconut** milk.

ناریل

coffee *noun*

Coffee is a drink. You make it by pouring hot water on **coffee** beans.

کافی

***Coffee** beans grow on a **coffee** plant.*

coin *noun*
coins

A **coin** is a round, flat piece of metal that is used as money.

سکہ

cold *adjective*
colder, coldest

1 If you are **cold**, you do not feel comfortable because you are not warm enough.

سردی لگنا، ٹھنڈک محسوس کرنا

*Wear a jumper if you are **cold**.*

2 If something is **cold**, it is not hot.

ٹھنڈا

*The weather is very **cold**.*

cold *noun*
colds

When you have a **cold**, you sneeze and cough a lot, and you have a sore throat.

نزلہ زکام میں مبتلا ہونا

collar *noun*
collars

1 The **collar** of a shirt or jacket is the part that goes around your neck.

کالر

2 A **collar** is also a band that goes around the neck of a dog or cat.

پٹہ، پالتو جانور کے گردن میں لگی پٹی نما شے

collect *verb*
collects, collecting, collected
1 If you **collect** things, you bring them together.
جمع کرنا
*He **collected** wood for the fire.*
2 If you **collect** someone from a place, you go there and take them away.
لے جانا
*Mum **collected** us from school.*

colour *noun*
colours
Red, blue and yellow are the main **colours**. You can mix them together to make other **colours**.
رنگ

comb *noun*
combs

A **comb** is a flat piece of metal or plastic with very thin points that you use to make your hair tidy.
کنگھی / کنگھا

come *verb*
comes, coming, came, come
When you **come** to a place, you move towards it or arrive there.
آنا
*She **came** into the room.*

comfortable *adjective*
If something is **comfortable**, it makes you feel good.
آرام دہ
*This is a very **comfortable** chair.*

comic *noun*
comics
A **comic** is a magazine with stories that are told in pictures.

بالتصویر کہانی

common *adjective*
If things are **common**, you see lots of them around, or they happen often.
عمومی
*Foxes are quite **common** in this area.*

compact disc *noun*
compact discs
A **compact disc** is a round, flat piece of plastic that has music or information on it. **Compact discs** are also called CDs.
کمپیکٹ ڈسک

competition *noun*
competitions
When you are in a **competition**, you try to show that you are the best at something.
مقابلہ
*She won the painting **competition**.*

complete *adjective*
If something is **complete**, none of it is missing.
مکمل
*He had a **complete** set of crayons.*

computer *noun*
computers

A **computer** is a machine that can store a lot of information and can work things out very quickly.
کمپیوٹر
*We played games on our **computer**.*

confused *adjective*
If you are **confused**, you do not understand what is happening, or you do not know what to do.
متذبذب
*She was **confused** about where to go.*

consonant *noun*
consonants
A **consonant** is any letter of the alphabet that is not a, e, i, o, or u.
حرف صحیح
*The word "book" has two **consonants** in it.*

container *noun*
containers
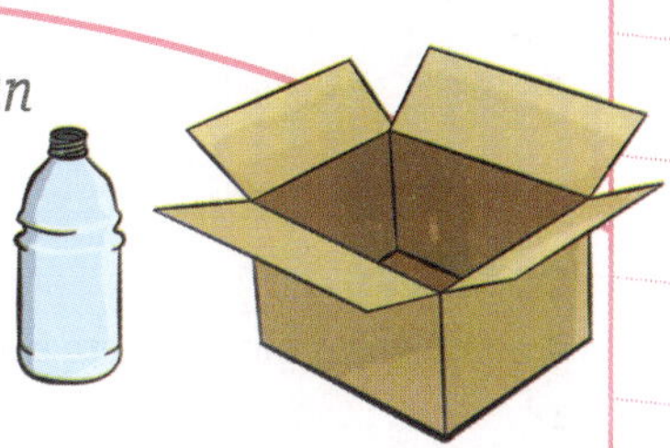
A **container** is something that you use to keep things in, for example a box or a bottle.
ڈبہ

A B C D E F G H I J K L M N O P Q R S T U V W X Y Z

control *verb*
controls, controlling, controlled
If you **control** something, you can make it do what you want.
قابو میں رکھنا
*I can **control** the speed by pressing this button.*

cook *verb*
cooks, cooking, cooked
When you **cook** food, you make it hot and get it ready to eat.
پکانا
*Mum was **cooking** dinner.*

cooker *noun*
cookers
A **cooker** is a machine that you use to cook food.
کوکر

cool *adjective*
cooler, coolest
Something that is **cool** is quite cold.
ٹھنڈا، ٹھنڈا کرنا
*Put the milk in the fridge to keep it **cool**.*

copy *noun*
copies
A **copy** is something that is made to look like another thing.
نقل کرنا
*I made a **copy** of the drawing.*

corn *noun*
Corn is a long vegetable. It is covered with yellow seeds that you eat.
مکئی

corner *noun*
corners
A **corner** is a place where two sides join together.
کونہ
*He stood at the **corner** of the street.*

correct *adjective*
If something is **correct**, there are no mistakes in it.
درست، صحیح

cost *noun*
costs
The **cost** of something is the amount of money you need to buy it.
لاگت، قیمت
*The **cost** of the holiday was too high.*

cot *noun*
cots
A **cot** is a bed for a baby, with high sides to stop the baby from falling out.
پلنگڑی، کھٹولا

cotton *noun*
1 **Cotton** is a kind of cloth that is made from the **cotton** plant.
سوتی
2 **Cotton** is also thread that you use to sew with.
سوتی دھاگہ

cough *verb*
coughs, coughing, coughed
When you **cough**, you make air come out of your throat with a sudden, loud noise.
کھانسی
*The smoke made us **cough**.*

could *verb*
If you say you **could** do something, you mean that you were able to do it. **Could** comes from the word **can**.
کر سکنا، کرنے کے قابل ہونا
*I **could** see through the window.*

couldn't
Couldn't is short for **could not**.
نہیں کر سکنا، کرنے کے قابل نہ ہونا
*She **couldn't** open the door.*

count *verb*
counts, counting, counted

1 When you **count**, you say numbers in order, one after the other.
گنتی کرنا
*I **counted** from one to ten.*

2 When you **count** all the things in a group, you add them up to see how many there are.
شمار کرنا، گنتی کرنا
*The teacher **counted** the children in the class.*

country *noun*
countries

1 A **country** is a part of the world with its own people and laws.
ملک
*He lives in a different **country**.*

2 The **country** is land that is away from towns and cities. There are farms and woods in the **country**.
دیہی علاقہ
*We went for a walk in the **country**.*

cousin *noun*
cousins

Your **cousin** is the son or daughter of your uncle or aunt.
چچازاد بھائی یا بہن

cover *verb*
covers, covering, covered

If you **cover** something, you put another thing over it.
ڈھکنا
*She **covered** the table with a cloth.*

cover *noun*
covers

A **cover** is something that you put over another thing.
خول، ڈھکن
*Put a **cover** over the sofa to keep it clean.*

cow *noun*
cows

A **cow** is a large animal that is kept on farms because it gives milk.
گائے

crab *noun*
crabs

A **crab** is an animal with a hard shell that lives in the sea. **Crabs** have large claws on their front legs.
کیکڑا

crack *verb*
cracks, cracking, cracked

If something **cracks**, it becomes damaged, and lines appear on the surface where it has broken.
دراڑ پڑ جانا
*The window **cracked**.*

crane *noun*
cranes

1 A **crane** is a tall machine that can lift very heavy things.
کرین

2 A **crane** is also a large bird with a long neck and long legs. **Cranes** live near water.
سارس، بگلا

crash *noun*
crashes

1 A **crash** is an accident when a vehicle hits something.
ٹکر
*There was a car **crash** outside the school.*

2 A **crash** is also a sudden, loud noise.
تیز آواز
*He dropped the plates with a **crash**.*

crawl *verb*
crawls, crawling, crawled

When you **crawl**, you move along on your hands and knees.
رینگنا
*The baby **crawled** along the floor.*

crayon *noun*
crayons

Crayons are pencils or sticks of wax in different colours that you use for drawing.
رنگین مومی پینسل

cream *noun*

Cream is a thick liquid that is made from milk. You can use it in cooking or pour it over puddings.
کریم، ملائی

a b c d e f g h i j k l m n o p q r s t u v w x y z

creature *noun*
creatures
A **creature** is anything that is alive, but is not a plant.
جاندار
*Many **creatures** live in the forest.*

creep *verb*
creeps, creeping, crept
1 If you **creep** somewhere, you move in a very slow and quiet way.
دھیرے دھیرے چلنا
*He **crept** up the stairs.*
2 If an animal **creeps**, it moves along close to the ground.
رینگنا
*The mouse **crept** across the room.*

crew *noun*
crews
A **crew** is a group of people who work together on a ship or an aeroplane.
عملہ

cricket *noun*
crickets
1 **Cricket** is a game where two teams take turns to hit a ball with a bat and run up and down.
کرکٹ
2 A **cricket** is also a small jumping insect that rubs its wings together to make a high sound.
جھینگر

cried
➪ Look at **cry**.
*The baby **cried** for its mother.*

cries
➪ Look at **cry**.
*She always **cries** at sad films.*

crocodile *noun*
crocodiles
A **crocodile** is a large reptile with a long body, a long mouth and sharp teeth. **Crocodiles'** mouths are in the shape of a letter V.
مگرمچھ

crop *noun*
crops
Crops are plants that people grow for food, for example potatoes and wheat.
فصل

cross *verb*
crosses, crossing, crossed
If you **cross** something, you go from one side of it to the other.
پار کرنا
***Cross** the road where it is safe.*

cross *noun*
crosses
A **cross** is a mark that you write. It looks like ×.
کاٹنے کا نشان
*She put a **cross** beside my name.*

cross *adjective*
crosser, crossest
If you are **cross**, you feel angry about something.
غصہ
*Mum was **cross** because we were late.*

crowd *noun*
crowds
A **crowd** is a lot of people together in one place.
بھیڑ
*A big **crowd** came to see the game.*

crown *noun*
crowns
A **crown** is a circle made of gold or silver and jewels that kings and queens wear on their heads.
تاج

cry *verb*
cries, crying, cried
When you **cry**, tears come from your eyes. People **cry** when they are sad or hurt.
رونا
*The baby started to **cry**.*

cry *noun*
cries
A **cry** is a loud sound that you make with your voice.
چیخ
*I heard the **cry** of a bird.*

cub *noun*
cubs
A **cub** is a young wild animal, for example a young bear or lion.
شیر کا بچہ

cube *noun*
cubes
A **cube** is a solid shape with six sides that are all squares.
مکعب
*A dice is in the shape of a **cube**.*

cucumber *noun*
cucumbers
A **cucumber** is a long, thin, green vegetable that you eat in salads.
کھیرا

cuddle *verb*
cuddles, cuddling, cuddled
If you **cuddle** someone, you put your arms around them and hold them close to you.
گلے لگانا

cup *noun*
cups

A **cup** is a small, round container with a handle. You drink things like tea and coffee from a **cup**.
پیالی

cupboard *noun*
cupboards
A **cupboard** is a piece of furniture with a door and shelves that you keep things in.
الماری
*The **cupboard** was full of toys.*

curl *noun*
curls
A **curl** is a piece of hair that has a curved shape.
خم
*The girl had long, black **curls**.*

curtain *noun*
curtains
A **curtain** is a piece of cloth that you pull across a window to cover it.
پردہ

curved *adjective*
If something is **curved**, it has the shape of a bent line.
مڑا ہونا، کمان کی طرح مڑا ہونا
*The bird had a **curved** beak.*

cushion *noun*
cushions
A **cushion** is a bag of soft material that you put on a seat to make it more comfortable.
گدا

customer *noun*
customers
A **customer** is a person who buys something in a shop.
خریدار، صارف

cut *verb*
cuts, cutting, cut
1 If you **cut** something, you use a knife or scissors to divide it into pieces.
کاٹنا
*We **cut** the cake.*
2 If you **cut** yourself, something sharp goes through your skin and blood comes out.
کاٹ لینا
*Don't **cut** yourself on the broken glass.*

cut *noun*
cuts
A **cut** is a place on your skin where something sharp has gone through it.
کٹنے کا زخم
*He had a **cut** on his cheek.*

A B C D E F G H I J K L M N O P Q R S T U V W X Y Z

Dd

dad or **daddy** *noun*
dads or **daddies**

Dad or **daddy** is a name for your father.

والد، ابا، ابو، اباجی، پاپا، ڈیڈی

damage *verb*
damages, damaging, damaged

If you **damage** something, you break it or spoil it.

نقصان پہنچانا، تباہ ہونا

*The storm **damaged** the roof.*

damp *adjective*
damper, dampest

Something that is **damp** is a little bit wet.

نم

*Her hair was **damp**.*

dance *verb*
dances, dancing, danced

When you **dance**, you move your body to music.

رقص کرنا، ناچنا

danger *noun*
dangers

If there is **danger**, something bad might happen to hurt you.

خطرہ

*There is a **danger** that he will fall.*

dangerous *adjective*

If something is **dangerous**, it can hurt you or kill you.

خطرناک

*It is **dangerous** to cross the road here.*

dark *adjective*
darker, darkest

1 When it is **dark**, there is no light or not much light.

اندھیرا

2 A **dark** colour is not pale.

گہرا

*She wore a **dark** blue skirt.*

date *noun*
dates

A **date** is the day, the month, and sometimes the year when something happens.

تاریخ

*What **date** is your birthday?*

daughter *noun*
daughters

Someone's **daughter** is their female child.

بیٹی

day *noun*
days

1 A **day** is the length of time between one midnight and the next. There are twenty-four hours in a **day**, and seven **days** in a week.

روز، دن

*It is three **days** until my birthday.*

2 **Day** is the time when there is light outside.

دن

*I've been busy all **day**.*

dead *adjective*

A person, an animal, or a plant that is **dead** has stopped living.

مردہ

deaf *adjective*

Someone who is **deaf** cannot hear anything, or cannot hear very well.

بہرا

December *noun*

December is the month after November and before January. It has 31 days.

دسمبر

decide *verb*
decides, deciding, decided

When you **decide** to do something, you think about it and then choose to do it.

فیصلہ کرنا

*She **decided** to go home.*

decorate *verb*
decorates, decorating, decorated

If you **decorate** a room, you put paint or paper on its walls.

آرائش کرنا، آراستہ کرنا

*We **decorated** the bedroom.*

deep *adjective*
deeper, deepest

If something is **deep**, it goes down a long way.

گہرا

*We dug a **deep** hole in the sand.*

deer *noun*
deer

A **deer** is a large animal that lives in forests and can run very fast. Male **deer** have big horns that look like branches on their heads.

ہرن

defend *verb*
defends, defending, defended

If you **defend** someone, you keep them safe from danger.

دفاع کرنا

*The soldiers **defended** the king.*

delicious *adjective*

If food is **delicious**, it tastes or smells very good.

لذیذ

deliver *verb*
delivers, delivering, delivered

If you **deliver** something, you take it to someone.

سونپنا

*Please **deliver** this letter to him.*

dentist *noun*
dentists

A **dentist** is a person whose job is to take care of people's teeth.

معالج دندان

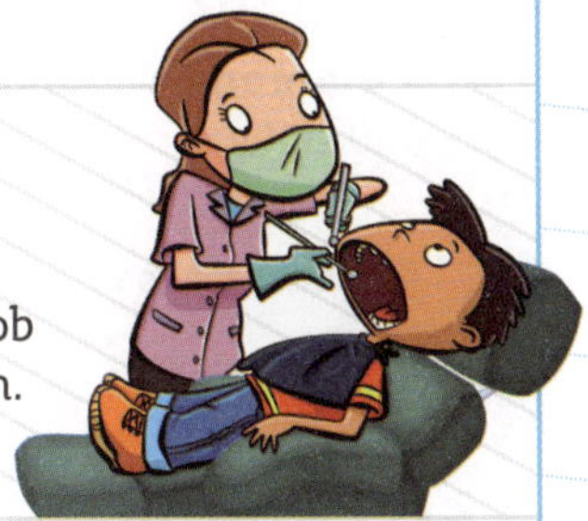

depth *noun*
depths

The **depth** of something is how far down it goes from its top to its bottom.

گہرائی

*The **depth** of the pond is two metres.*

describe *verb*
describes, describing, described

If you **describe** something, you say what it is like.

بیان کرنا

*He **described** the picture to me.*

desert *noun*
deserts

A **desert** is a large, dry area of land with almost no trees or plants. **Deserts** are very hot and are often covered with sand.

ریگستان

desk *noun*
desks

A **desk** is a kind of table that you sit at to write or to work.

لکھنے کی میز

destroy *verb*
destroys, destroying, destroyed

If you **destroy** something, you damage it so much that it cannot be used any more.

برباد کرنا

*The fire **destroyed** the house.*

diagram *noun*
diagrams
A **diagram** is a drawing that shows something in a way that is very easy to understand.
خاکہ
*He drew me a **diagram** of the engine.*

diamond *noun*
diamonds
1 A **diamond** is a kind of jewel that is hard, clear, and shiny.
ہیرا
2 A **diamond** is also a shape with four straight sides.
چوکور

diary *noun*
diaries
A **diary** is a book that you use to write down things that happen to you each day.
ڈائری، بیاض

dice *noun*
dice
A **dice** is a small cube with a different number of spots on each side. You throw **dice** in some games.
پانسہ

dictionary *noun*
dictionaries
A **dictionary** is a book with a list of words in it. The **dictionary** tells you what these words mean, and shows you how to spell them.
لغت

did
⇨ Look at **do**.
*I saw what you **did**.*

didn't
Didn't is short for **did not**.
نہیں کرنا
*She **didn't** like the film.*

die *verb*
dies, dying, died
When a person, an animal, or a plant **dies**, they stop living.
مرنا
*Plants **die** if you don't water them.*

different *adjective*
If two things are **different**, they are not like each other.
مختلف
*The crayons were all in **different** colours.*

difficult *adjective*
If something is **difficult**, it is not easy to do or to understand.
مشکل
*The homework was too **difficult** for us.*

dig *verb*
digs, digging, dug
If you **dig**, you make a hole in the ground.
کھودنا
*We **dug** a hole in the garden.*

digital *adjective*
If a machine is **digital**, it shows or sends information by using numbers.
ہندسی، ڈیجیٹل
*We have a new **digital** television.*

dinner *noun*
dinners
Dinner is the main meal of the day.
عشائیہ

dinosaur *noun*
dinosaurs

Dinosaurs were large animals that lived a very long time ago. **Dinosaurs** were like very big lizards.

ڈائنا سور

direction *noun*
directions

1 A **direction** is the way that you go to get to a place.

سمت

*My house is in this **direction**.*

2 **Directions** are words or pictures that show you how to do something, or how to get somewhere.

ہدایت

*He gave me **directions** to the station.*

dirt *noun*

Dirt is anything that is not clean, for example, dust or mud.

گندگی

*She had **dirt** on her face.*

dirty *adjective*
dirtier, dirtiest

If something is **dirty**, it has mud, food, or other marks on it.

گندا

*The dishes were **dirty**.*

disappear *verb*
disappears, disappearing, disappeared

If something **disappears**, you cannot see it any more.

غائب ہونا

*The cat **disappeared** under the bed.*

disappointed *adjective*

If you are **disappointed**, you are sad because something you hoped for did not happen.

مایوس

*I was **disappointed** that you weren't there.*

disaster *noun*
disasters

A **disaster** is something very bad that happens suddenly and that may hurt many people.

بلا، حادثہ

discover *verb*
discovers, discovering, discovered

When you **discover** something, you get to know about it for the first time.

دریافت کرنا

*We **discovered** that he was very good at football.*

discuss *verb*
discusses, discussing, discussed

When people **discuss** something, they talk about it together.

مباحثہ کرنا

*We **discussed** what to do next.*

disease *noun*
diseases

A **disease** is something that makes you ill.

بیماری

*Measles is a **disease**.*

disguise *noun*
disguises

A **disguise** is something you wear so that people will not know who you are.

بہروپ بھرنا

dish *noun*
dishes

A **dish** is a container that you use to cook or serve food in.

طشتری، تھالی

disk *noun*
disks

A **disk** is a flat piece of metal and plastic that you use in a computer to store information.

ڈسک (ہارڈ ڈسک)

distance *noun*
distances
The **distance** between two things is how much space there is between them.
فاصلہ
*Measure the **distance** between the wall and the table.*

dive *verb*
dives, diving, dived
If you **dive** into water, you jump in so that your arms and your head go in first.
غوطہ لگانا، ڈبکی لگانا

divide *verb*
divides, dividing, divided
1 If you **divide** something, you make it into smaller pieces.
تقسیم کرنا
***Divide** the cake into four pieces.*
2 When you **divide** numbers, you see how many times one number goes into another number.
تقسیم کرنا
*If you **divide** ten by five, you get two.*

do *verb*
does, doing, did, done
If you **do** something, you spend some time on it or finish it.
کرنا
*I tried to **do** some work.*

doctor *noun*
doctors
A **doctor** is a person whose job is to help people who are ill or hurt to get better.
ڈاکٹر

does
⇨ Look at **do**.
*She **does** her homework before dinner.*

doesn't
Doesn't is short for **does not**.
نہیں کرنا
*He **doesn't** like carrots.*

dog *noun*
dogs
A **dog** is an animal that barks. Some **dogs** do special jobs, like helping blind people.
کتا

doing
⇨ Look at **do**.
*What are you **doing**?*

doll *noun*
dolls
A **doll** is a toy that looks like a small person or a baby.
گڑیا

dolphin *noun*
dolphins
A **dolphin** is an animal that lives in the sea and looks like a large fish with a long nose. **Dolphins** are very clever.
ڈولفن مچھلی

done
⇨ Look at **do**.
*She has **done** a drawing.*

donkey *noun*
donkeys
A **donkey** is an animal that looks like a small horse with long ears.
گدھا

don't

Don't is short for **do not**.

نہ کرو، مت کرو

*I **don't** feel well.*

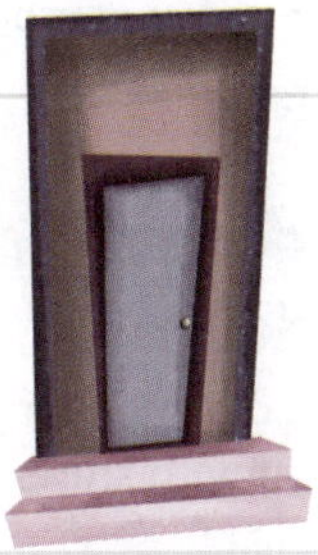

door *noun*

doors

You open and close a **door** to get into a building, a room, or a cupboard.

دروازہ

double *adjective*

Double means two times as big, or two times as much.

دوگنا، دُگنا

*His room is **double** the size of mine.*

down

When something moves **down**, it goes from a higher place to a lower place.

نیچے

*She came **down** the stairs.*

drag *verb*

drags, dragging, dragged

If you **drag** something, you pull it along the ground.

گھسیٹنا

*He **dragged** his chair to the table.*

dragon *noun*

dragons

In stories, a **dragon** is a monster that has wings and can make fire come out of its mouth.

اژدہا

drain *verb*

drains, draining, drained

If you **drain** a liquid, you take it away by making it flow to another place.

بہا دینا

*They **drained** the water out of the tunnel.*

drank

⇨ Look at **drink**.

*She **drank** a bottle of water.*

draw *verb*

draws, drawing, drew, drawn

When you **draw**, you use pens, pencils, or crayons to make a picture.

کھینچنا، خاکہ بنانا

*He likes to **draw** animals.*

drawer *noun*

drawers

A **drawer** is a box that fits inside a piece of furniture. You can pull it out and put things in it.

دراز

drawing *noun*

drawings

A **drawing** is a picture you make with pens, pencils, or crayons.

خاکہ

drawn

⇨ Look at **draw**.

*I have **drawn** my house.*

dream *noun*

dreams

A **dream** is something you see and hear in your mind while you are sleeping.

خواب

*I had a **dream** about winning the prize.*

dress *noun*

dresses

A **dress** is something a girl or a woman can wear. It covers the body and part of the legs.

لباس

*She wore a yellow **dress**.*

A B C D E F G H I J K L M N O P Q R S T U V W X Y Z

dress *verb*
dresses, dressing, dressed
When you **dress**, you put on clothes.
لباس پہننا
*He **dressed** quickly because he was late.*

drew
⇨ Look at **draw**.
*She **drew** a picture of a horse.*

drink *verb*
drinks, drinking, drank, drunk
When you **drink**, you swallow liquid.
پینا
*Mum **drinks** a lot of coffee.*

drip *verb*
drips, dripping, dripped
When liquid **drips**, a small amount of it falls from somewhere.
ٹپکنا
*Water **dripped** from the roof.*

drive *verb*
drives, driving, drove, driven
When someone **drives** a vehicle, they make it go where they want.
گاڑی چلانا
*He knows how to **drive** a car.*

drop *verb*
drops, dropping, dropped
If you **drop** something, you let it fall.
گرانا
*I **dropped** a plate on the floor.*

drove
⇨ Look at **drive**.
*We **drove** to the shops.*

drown *verb*
drowns, drowning, drowned
If someone **drowns**, they die because their face is below water and they cannot breathe.
ڈوبنا

drum *noun*
drums
A **drum** is an instrument that you hit with sticks or with your hands to make music.
ڈھول

drunk
⇨ Look at **drink**.
*Have you **drunk** all the milk?*

dry *adjective*
drier, driest
If something is **dry**, there is no water in it or on it.
خشک، سوکھا
*My clothes are **dry**.*

duck *noun*
ducks
A **duck** is a bird that lives near water and can swim. **Ducks** have large flat beaks.
بطخ

dug
⇨ Look at **dig**.
*We **dug** a hole in the sand.*

dull *adjective*
duller, dullest
1 Something that is **dull** is not interesting.
بیزار کن، پھیکا
*That was a very **dull** book.*
2 A **dull** colour is not bright.
مدھم، ہلکا
*He wore a **dull** green jacket.*

dust *noun*
Dust is tiny pieces of dry dirt that looks like powder.
دھول، غبار
*The table was covered in **dust**.*

Ee

each

Each means every one.

ہر ایک

*He gave **each** of us a book.*

eagle *noun*

eagles

An **eagle** is a large bird with a curved beak and sharp claws. **Eagles** eat small animals.

باز

ear *noun*

ears

Your **ears** are the two parts of your body that you hear sounds with.

کان

*He whispered something in her **ear**.*

early *adjective*

earlier, earliest

1 If you are **early**, you arrive before the time that you were expected to come.

سویرے

*She was too **early** for the party.*

2 **Early** also means near the first part of something.

صبح سویرے

*I got up **early** in the morning.*

earn *verb*

earns, earning, earned

If you **earn** money, you work to get it.

کما

*He **earned** some money washing the car.*

earth *noun*

1 The **Earth** is the planet that we live on.

زمین

2 **Earth** is also the soil that plants grow in.

مٹی

earthquake *noun*

earthquakes

When there is an **earthquake**, the ground shakes and buildings often fall down.

زلزلہ

east *noun*

The **east** is the direction that is in front of you when you are looking towards the place where the sun rises.

مشرق، پورب

easy *adjective*

easier, easiest

If something is **easy**, you can do it or understand it without having to try very much.

آسان

*These sums are **easy**.*

eat *verb*

eats, eating, ate, eaten

When you **eat**, you chew and swallow food.

کھانا

*She **eats** too many sweets.*

echo *noun*

echoes

An **echo** is a sound that you hear again because it bounces off something solid and then comes back.

بازگشت

*We heard the **echo** of our voices in the cave.*

A B C D E F G H I J K L M N O P Q R S T U V W X Y Z

edge *noun*
edges
The **edge** of something is the part along the end or side of it.
کنارا
*She stood at the **edge** of the pond.*

effect *noun*
effects
An **effect** is something that happens because of another thing.
اثر
*The flood was an **effect** of all the rain.*

effort *noun*
efforts
If you make an **effort** to do something, you have to work a lot to do it.
کوشش
*She made an **effort** to win the race.*

egg *noun*
eggs
Baby birds, insects, and some other animals live in **eggs** until they are big enough to come out and be born. People often eat hens' **eggs** as food.
انڈا

eight *noun*
Eight is the number **8**.
آٹھ

elbow *noun*
elbows
Your **elbow** is the part in the middle of your arm where it bends.
کہنی
*She put her **elbows** on the table.*

electricity *noun*
Electricity is a kind of energy that is used to make light, to make things hot, and to make machines work.
برق

elephant *noun*
elephants
An **elephant** is a very large, grey animal with big ears, a long nose called a trunk, and two long, curved teeth called tusks.
ہاتھی

eleven *noun*
Eleven is the number **11**.
گیارہ

email or **e-mail** *noun*
An **email** is a message like a letter that you send from one computer to another.
ای میل
*I got an **email** from my cousin.*

empty *adjective*
emptier, emptiest
If something is **empty**, there is nothing inside it.
خالی
*The bottle was **empty**.*

encyclopedia *noun*
encyclopedias
An **encyclopedia** is a book that gives you information about many different things.
قاموس، انسائیکلوپیڈیا، ایک کتاب جس میں متعدد مختلف چیزوں کے بارے میں معلومات درج ہوں

end *noun*
ends
The **end** of something is the last part of it.
سرا، اختتامی حصہ
*He told me the **end** of the story.*

enemy *noun*
enemies
If someone is your **enemy**, they hate you and want to hurt you.
دشمن

energy *noun*

1 If you have **energy**, you have the strength to move around a lot and do things.
توانائی
*He has the **energy** to run for miles.*

2 **Energy** is also the power that makes machines work.
توانائی
*The lamp gets its **energy** from the sun.*

engine *noun*
engines

1 An **engine** is a machine that makes things like cars and planes move.
انجن

2 An **engine** is also the front part of a train that pulls it along.
انجن

enjoy *verb*
enjoys, enjoying, enjoyed
If you **enjoy** something, you like doing it.
لطف اندوز ہونا
*I **enjoy** reading.*

enormous *adjective*
Something that is **enormous** is very big.
عظیم
*Whales are **enormous**.*

enough
If you have **enough** of something, you have as much as you need.
کافی، حسب ضرورت
*I don't have **enough** money to buy both books.*

enter *verb*
enters, entering, entered
When you **enter** a place, you go into it.
داخل ہونا

entrance *noun*
entrances
The **entrance** of a place is the way you get into it.
دروازہ
*We found the **entrance** to the tunnel.*

envelope *noun*
envelopes
An **envelope** is a paper cover that you put a letter or a card into before you send it to someone.
لفافہ

environment *noun*
The **environment** is the land, water, and air around us.
ماحول
*We must try to protect the **environment**.*

equal *adjective*
If two things are **equal**, they are the same in size, number, or amount.
مساوی، برابر
*Mix **equal** amounts of milk and water.*

equipment *noun*
Equipment is all the things that you need to do something.
سازوسامان
*He put his football **equipment** in his bag.*

escape *verb*
escapes, escaping, escaped
If a person or an animal **escapes**, they get away from somewhere.
فرار ہونا، بھاگ جانا
*My guinea pig **escaped** from its cage.*

even *adjective*

1 An **even** number is a number that you can divide by two, with nothing left over.
جفت عدد، برابر
*Four is an **even** number.*

2 Something that is **even** is flat and smooth.
ہموار
*The path was straight and **even**.*

evening *noun*
evenings
The **evening** is the part of each day between the end of the afternoon and the time when people usually go to bed.
شام

ever
Ever means at any time.
کبھی
*Have you **ever** seen anything like it?*

every *adjective*
You use **every** to mean all the people or things in a group.
سبھی
***Every** pupil in the school was there.*

everybody
Everybody means all the people in a group, or all the people in the world.
ہر کوئی
***Everybody** likes him.*

everyone
Everyone means all the people in a group, or all the people in the world.
ہر ایک
***Everyone** knows who she is.*

everything
Everything means all of something.
سب کچھ
*He told me **everything** that happened.*

everywhere
Everywhere means in every place.
جگہ
*I looked **everywhere** for my keys.*

example *noun*
examples
An **example** is something that you use to show what other things in the same group are like.
مثال
*Here is an **example** of my drawings.*

excellent *adjective*
Something that is **excellent** is very good.
بہت خوب
*It was an **excellent** film.*

excited *adjective*
If you are **excited**, you are very happy about something and you keep thinking about it.
مشتعل
*He was very **excited** about going to the beach.*

excuse *noun*
excuses
An **excuse** is a reason that you give to explain why you did something.
وجہ معذرت
*She had a good **excuse** for being late.*

exercise *noun*
exercises
1 When you do **exercise**, you move your body so that you can keep healthy and strong.
ورزش، کثرت
*Running and swimming are both good **exercise**.*
2 An **exercise** is also something you do to practise what you have learnt.
مشق
*We did a maths **exercise**.*

exit *noun*
exits
The **exit** of a building is the door you use to get out of it.
نکاسی
*We left by the nearest **exit**.*

expect *verb*
expects, expecting, expected
If you **expect** something to happen, you think that it will happen.
توقع کرنا
*I **expect** that he will come.*

expensive *adjective*
If something is **expensive**, you need a lot of money to buy it.
مہنگا

explain *verb*
explains, explaining, explained
If you **explain** something, you talk about it so that people can understand it.
مطلب بتانا
*He **explained** to me how the machine worked.*

explode *verb*
explodes, exploding, exploded
If something **explodes**, it bursts with a very loud noise.
دھماکے سے پھٹنا

explore *verb*
explores, exploring, explored
If you **explore** a place, you look around it to see what it is like.
دریافتی سیاحت کرنا
*We **explored** the old castle.*

extinct *adjective*
If an animal or a plant is **extinct**, there are none of them alive any more.
نایاب
*Dinosaurs are **extinct**.*

extra *adjective*
Extra means more than the usual amount.
اضافی
*I wore an **extra** jumper because it was cold.*

eye *noun*
eyes
Your **eyes** are the parts of your body that you see with.
آنکھ
*I opened my **eyes** and looked.*

Ff

face *noun*
faces
Your **face** is the front part of your head.
چہرہ
*She has a beautiful **face**.*

fact *noun*
facts
A **fact** is something that you know is true.
حقیقت

factory *noun*
factories
A **factory** is a large building where people use machines to make things.
کارخانہ
*He works in a **factory** that makes computers.*

fail *verb*
fails, failing, failed
If you **fail**, you try to do something but you cannot do it.
ناکام ہونا
*She **failed** to find her lost keys.*

fair *adjective*
fairer, fairest
1 If something is **fair**, it seems right because it is the same for everyone.
منصفانہ
*It's not **fair** – he's got more than me!*
2 **Fair** hair is pale yellow in colour.
ہلکے پیلے رنگ کا

A B C D E F G H I J K L M N O P Q R S T U V W X Y Z

fairy *noun*
fairies
In stories, **fairies** are tiny creatures with wings who can do magic.
پری

fall *verb*
falls, falling, fell, fallen
If a person or thing **falls**, they move towards the ground suddenly by accident.
گرنا
*He **fell** off his bike.*

fallen
⇨ Look at **fall**.
*An apple had **fallen** from the tree.*

family *noun*
families
A **family** is a group of people made up of parents and their children. Aunts and uncles, cousins, grandmothers, and grandfathers are also part of your **family**.
خاندان

famous *adjective*
If someone is **famous**, a lot of people know who they are.
مشہور
*She wants to be rich and **famous**.*

far
farther, farthest
If something is **far** away, it is a long way away.
دور
*His house was **far** away.*

farm *noun*
farms
A **farm** is a piece of land with buildings on it where people grow crops and keep animals.
فارم (کھیت مع گھر)

farmer *noun*
farmers
A **farmer** is a person who grows crops and keeps animals on a farm.
کسان

fast *adjective*
faster, fastest
Something that is **fast** can move quickly.
تیز
*This car is very **fast**.*

fasten *verb*
fastens, fastening, fastened
When you **fasten** something, you close it up.
باندھنا
*She **fastened** the buttons on her coat.*

fat *adjective*
fatter, fattest
Someone who is **fat** has a big, round body.
موٹا

father *noun*
fathers
A **father** is a man who has a child.
باپ

fault *noun*
faults
If something bad is your **fault**, you made it happen.
قصور
*It's my **fault** that we were late.*

favourite *adjective*
Your **favourite** person or thing is the one you like best.
پسندیدہ
*My **favourite** food is cheese.*

fear *noun*
Fear is the way you feel when you think that something bad is going to happen to you.
خوف، ڈر
*She shook with **fear**.*

feast *noun*
feasts
A **feast** is a large and special meal for a lot of people.
دعوت

feather *noun*
feathers
Feathers are the soft, light things that cover a bird's body. They keep the bird warm and help it to fly.
پنکھ

February *noun*
February is the month after January and before March. It usually has 28 days, but once every four years, it has 29 days.
فروری

feed *verb*
feeds, feeding, fed
If you **feed** a person or an animal, you give them food.
کھلانا، پلانا
*I **feed** my cat twice a day.*

feel *verb*
feels, feeling, felt
1 The way you **feel**, for example happy or sad, or cold or tired, is how you are at the time.
احساس
*I **feel** very upset.*
2 If you **feel** something, you touch it with your hand to see what it is like.
محسوس کرنا
***Feel** how soft these feathers are.*

feet
➡ Look at **foot**.
*Don't put your **feet** on the chair.*

fell
➡ Look at **fall**.
*She **fell** and hurt her knee.*

felt
➡ Look at **feel**.
*I **felt** angry.*

female *adjective*
A **female** person or animal could become a mother.
عورت، خاتون

fence *noun*
fences
A **fence** is a wall made of wood or metal that goes round a piece of land.
جنگلا، باڑا
*There is a **fence** round the garden.*

fetch *verb*
fetches, fetching, fetched
If you **fetch** something, you go to where it is and bring it back.
جاکر لانا
*He **fetched** a towel from the bathroom.*

fever *noun*
fevers
If you have a **fever** when you are ill, your body is too hot.
بخار، حرارت

few
fewer, fewest
A **few** means some, but not many.
چند، تھوڑا
*She gave me a **few** sweets.*

A B C D E F G H I J K L M N O P Q R S T U V W X Y Z

field *noun*
fields
A **field** is a piece of land where people grow crops or keep animals.
کھیت

fierce *adjective*
fiercer, fiercest
A **fierce** animal is very angry and might attack you.
شدید
*That dog looks very **fierce**.*

fight *verb*
fights, fighting, fought
When people **fight**, they try to hurt each other.
جنگ کرنا، لڑنا
*Two boys started to **fight** in the playground.*

fill *verb*
fills, filling, filled
If you **fill** something, you put so much into it that you cannot get any more in.
بھرنا
*She **filled** her cup with tea.*

film *noun*
films
A **film** is a story told in moving pictures that you watch on a screen.
فلم (سنیما)

fin *noun*
fins
A **fin** is one of the thin, flat parts on a fish's body that help it to swim.
مچھلی کے پنکھ

find *verb*
finds, finding, found
If you **find** something that has been lost, you see it after you have been looking for it.
پانا
*I can't **find** my shoes.*

fine *adjective*
finer, finest
1 If you say that you are **fine**, you mean that you are well or happy.
ٹھیک ہونا
*I feel **fine** now.*
2 Something that is **fine** is very thin.
باریک
*She sewed the cloth with **fine** thread.*
3 When the weather is **fine**, it is dry and sunny.
اچھا ہونا
*It is a **fine** day.*

finger *noun*
fingers
Your **fingers** are the long thin parts at the end of each hand.
انگلی
*She put the ring on her **finger**.*

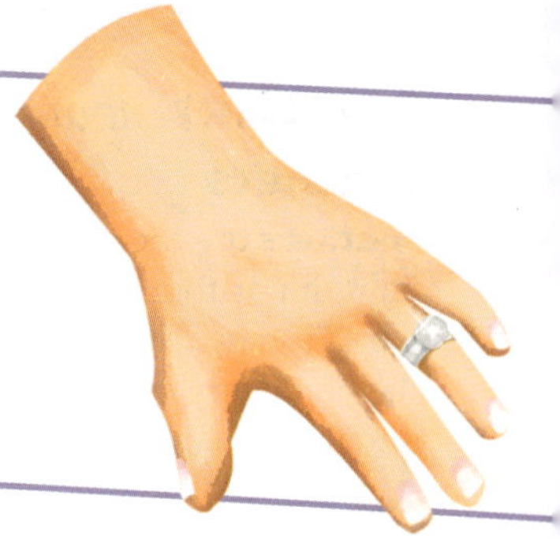

finish *verb*
finishes, finishing, finished
When you **finish** something, you come to the end of it.
ختم کرنا، مکمل کرنا
*I **finished** my homework.*

fire *noun*
fires
Fire is the hot, bright flames that come from something that is burning.
آگ
*The **fire** destroyed the forest.*

fire engine *noun*
fire engines
A **fire engine** is a large truck that carries people and equipment to stop fires.
آگ بجھانے والا ٹرک، فائر انجن

firework *noun*
fireworks
Fireworks are things that make a loud bang or flashes of bright colour when they are burned.
پٹاخے، بارود کا کام

firm *adjective*
firmer, firmest
Something that is **firm** is hard, and is not easy to bend.
مضبوط

first *adjective*
If a person or thing is **first**, they come before all the others.
پہلے
*January is the **first** month of the year.*

fish *noun*
fish, fishes
A **fish** is an animal that lives in water. **Fish** have fins to help them swim.
مچھلی

fit *verb*
fits, fitting, fitted
If something **fits** you, it is the right size and shape for you.
مناسب ہونا، موزوں ہونا
*These shoes don't **fit** me.*

five *noun*
Five is the number **5**.
پانچ

fix *verb*
fixes, fixing, fixed
1 If you **fix** something that is broken, you mend it.
ٹھیک کرنا
*He **fixed** the radio.*
2 If you **fix** something to another thing, you join them together.
لگانا، نصب کرنا
*She **fixed** the shelf to the wall.*

flag *noun*
flags
A **flag** is a piece of cloth with a pattern on it. Each country of the world has its own **flag**.
پرچم، جھنڈا

flame *noun*
flames
A **flame** is the hot, bright light that comes from a fire.
لپٹ
*The **flames** almost burned her fingers.*

flash *noun*
flashes
A **flash** is a sudden bright light.
تیز روشنی
*There was a **flash** of lightning.*

flat *adjective*
flatter, flattest
If something is **flat**, it is smooth and does not have any lumps.
ہموار، مسطح
*Lay the painting on a **flat** surface until it is dry.*

flavour *noun*
flavours
The **flavour** of food is the taste that it has.
ذائقہ، فلے ور
*They had ice cream in lots of **flavours**.*

flew
➡ Look at **fly**.
*An aeroplane **flew** across the sky.*

flies
➡ Look at **fly**.
*A bird **flies** by moving its wings.*

float *verb*
floats, floating, floated
1 If something **floats** in a liquid, it stays on top of it.
تیرنا
*The boat **floated** on the water.*
2 If something **floats** in the air, it moves slowly through it.
ہوا میں تیرنا، جھولنا
*A balloon **floated** over our heads.*

A B C D E F G H I J K L M N O P Q R S T U V W X Y Z

flock *noun*
flocks

A **flock** is the name for a group of birds or sheep.

جھنڈ

flood *noun*
floods

If there is a **flood**, a lot of water covers land that is usually dry.

سیلاب، باڑھ

*We couldn't get to school because of the **flood**.*

floor *noun*
floors

1 A **floor** is the part of a room that you walk on.

فرش

*There were carpets on the **floor**.*

2 A **floor** of a building is all the rooms in it that are at the same height.

منزل

*Our house is on the first **floor**.*

flour *noun*

Flour is a powder made from wheat that is used to make bread and cakes.

آٹا

flow *verb*
flows, flowing, flowed

If something **flows**, it moves along in a steady way and does not stop.

بہنا

*The river **flowed** through the forest.*

flower *noun*
flowers

A **flower** is the part of a plant that makes seeds. **Flowers** often have bright colours and a nice smell.

پھول

flown

➩ Look at **fly**.

*The birds have all **flown** away.*

flu *noun*

If you have **flu**, you feel as if you have a very bad cold, and your body aches.

فلو

fly *verb*
flies, flying, flew, flown

When a bird or aeroplane **flies**, it moves through the air.

اڑنا

fly *noun*
flies

A **fly** is a small insect with two thin, clear wings.

مکھی

fog *noun*

Fog is a thick cloud that is close to the ground. It is hard to see through it.

کہرا

fold *verb*
folds, folding, folded

If you **fold** something, you bend it so that one part of it goes over another.

موڑنا، تہ کرنا

*He **folded** the letter and put it in the envelope.*

follow *verb*
follows, following, followed

If you **follow** someone, you go along behind them.

تعاقب کرنا

*We **followed** him up the stairs.*

food *noun*
foods
Food is what people and animals eat.
کھانا، خوراک

foot *noun*
feet
Your **feet** are the parts of your body that are at the ends of your legs, and that you stand on.
پیر
*Stand with one **foot** in front of the other.*

football *noun*
footballs
1 **Football** is a game played by two teams of eleven people who kick a ball and try to score goals by getting the ball into a net.
فٹبال
2 A **football** is the ball that you use to play football.
بال

forehead *noun*
foreheads
Your **forehead** is the part of your face that is between your hair and your eyes.
پیشانی
*She had a bruise on her **forehead**.*

forest *noun*
forests
A **forest** is a place where a lot of trees grow close together.
جنگل

forever
If something goes on **forever**, it never comes to an end.
ہمیشہ کے لیے
*The film seemed to go on **forever**.*

forgave
⇨ Look at **forgive**.
*She **forgave** her brother for spoiling her drawing.*

forget *verb*
forgets, forgetting, forgot, forgotten
If you **forget** something, you do not remember it.
بھولنا
*Don't **forget** to lock the door.*

forgive *verb*
forgives, forgiving, forgave, forgiven
If you **forgive** someone who has done something bad, you stop being angry with them.
معاف کر دینا
*Please **forgive** me for being late.*

forgot
⇨ Look at **forget**.
*She **forgot** to bring any money.*

forgotten
⇨ Look at **forget**.
*I have **forgotten** my keys.*

fork *noun*
forks
A **fork** is a tool with three or four thin, sharp points that you use to eat food with.
کانٹا

fortnight *noun*
fortnights
A **fortnight** is two weeks.
پندرہ دن

forwards
If you move **forwards**, you move towards the front.
آگے
*They ran backwards and **forwards** trying to catch the ball.*

fought

⇨ Look at **fight**.

*The knights **fought** with swords.*

found

⇨ Look at **find**.

*She **found** her lost dog.*

four *noun*

Four is the number **4**.

چار

fox *noun*

foxes

A **fox** is an animal that looks like a dog with red fur and a long, thick tail.

لومڑی

fraction *noun*

fractions

A **fraction** is a part of a whole number.

کسر

*A half and a quarter are both **fractions**.*

frame *noun*

frames

A **frame** is a piece of wood, metal or plastic that fits around the edge of a picture, a window, or a door.

چوکھٹا

freckles *noun*

Freckles are light brown spots that some people have on their skin.

جھائیاں، جلد پر بھورے رنگ کے دھبے پڑ جانا

*His face was covered with **freckles**.*

free *adjective*

freer, freest

1 If something is **free**, you can have it without paying any money for it.

مفت

*If you buy a cup of coffee, you get a **free** cake.*

2 If you are **free**, you can do what you like or go where you like.

آزاد

*You are **free** to come here any time.*

freeze *verb*

freezes, freezing, froze, frozen

1 When water **freezes**, it is so cold that it becomes ice.

جمنا

2 If you **freeze** food, you make it very cold so that it will not go bad.

منجمد کرنا

fresh *adjective*

fresher, freshest

1 If food is **fresh**, it has been picked or made a short time ago.

تازہ

*Eat some **fresh** fruit every day.*

2 **Fresh** water has no salt in it. The water in rivers is **fresh**.

تازہ

3 **Fresh** air is clean and cool.

تازہ

Friday *noun*

Fridays

Friday is the day after Thursday and before Saturday.

جمعہ

*He went home on **Friday**.*

fridge *noun*

fridges

A **fridge** is a cupboard that uses electricity to keep food cold and fresh.

فرِج

*Put the butter in the **fridge**.*

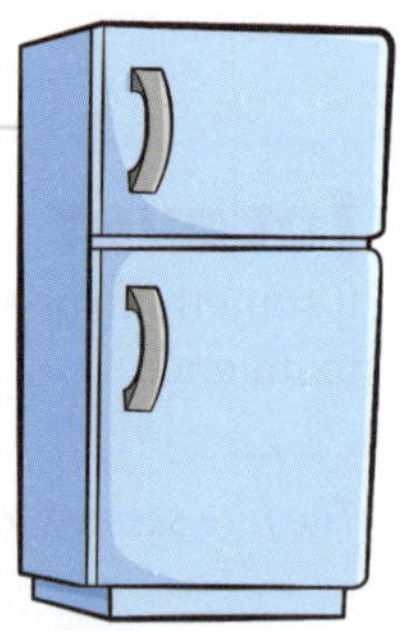

fried

➪ Look at **fry**.

*She **fried** some eggs.*

friend *noun*

friends

A **friend** is someone you know and like, and who likes you too.

دوست

friendly *adjective*

friendlier, friendliest

If someone is **friendly**, they like to meet other people, and are nice to them.

دوستانہ

frighten *verb*

frightens, frightening, frightened

If something **frightens** you, it makes you feel afraid.

ڈرنا، ڈرانا

*Loud noises **frighten** her.*

frog *noun*

frogs

A **frog** is a small animal with smooth skin, big eyes, and long back legs that it uses for jumping. **Frogs** live near water.

مینڈک

front *noun*

fronts

The **front** of something is the part that comes first or the part that you usually see first.

آگے

*She stood at the **front** of the queue.*

frost *noun*

Frost is ice that looks like white powder. It covers things outside when the weather is very cold.

انجماد

frown *verb*

frowns, frowning, frowned

When you **frown**, lines appear on your forehead because you are cross or because you are thinking about something.

تیوری چڑھانا

froze

➪ Look at **freeze**.

*It was so cold that the lake **froze**.*

frozen

➪ Look at **freeze**.

*The water had **frozen** into ice.*

fruit *noun*

fruits

Fruit is the part of a plant or a tree that has the seeds in it. You can eat many **fruits**, for example apples, bananas, and strawberries.

پھل

fry *verb*

fries, frying, fried

When you **fry** food, you cook it in hot oil or butter.

تلنا

***Fry** the onions until they are brown.*

full *adjective*

fuller, fullest

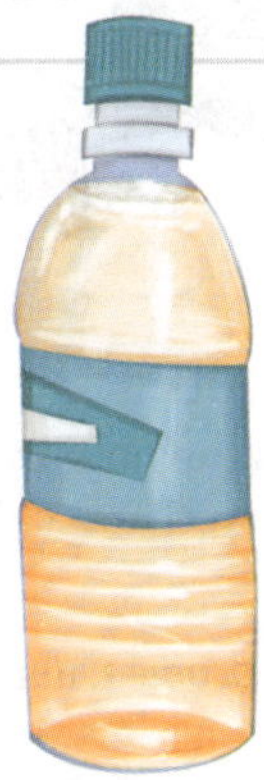

If something is **full**, it has so much in it that it cannot hold any more.

لبریز

*The bottle is **full**.*

A B C D E F G H I J K L M N O P Q R S T U V W X Y Z

fun *noun*
When you have **fun**, you enjoy doing something and you feel happy.
تفریح، موج مستی
*They had **fun** at the beach.*

funny *adjective*
funnier, funniest
1 If something is **funny**, it makes you laugh.
پر مزاح، ہنسانے والا
*He told me a **funny** joke.*
2 **Funny** also means strange.
عجیب
*The car is making a **funny** noise.*

fur *noun*
Fur is the soft hair that covers the bodies of many animals.
پشم، بال
*Pandas have black and white **fur**.*

furniture *noun*
Furniture is the name for all the big things, for example tables, chairs, or beds, that people have in their houses.
فرنیچر، کرسی میز وغیرہ
*We bought new **furniture** for the bedroom.*

future *noun*
The **future** is the time that will come after the present time.
آئندہ
*In the **future**, people will travel to other planets.*

Gg

gale *noun*
gales
A **gale** is a very strong wind.
جھکڑ

game *noun*
games
1 A **game** is something you play that has rules, for example football.
کھیل، گیم
2 Children also play a **game** when they pretend to be other people.
گیم، کھیل
*We played a **game** of pirates.*

gap *noun*
gaps
A **gap** is a space between two things.
شگاف
*There was a **gap** between the curtains.*

garage *noun*
garages
1 A **garage** is a building where you keep a car.
گیراج، کار کھڑی کرنے کی جگہ
2 A **garage** is also a place where you can get your car repaired.
گیراج، کار مرمت کرنے کی جگہ

garden *noun*
gardens
A **garden** is a piece of land near a house where people can grow grass, flowers, and vegetables.
باغیچہ

gas *noun*
gases
A **gas** is anything, for example air, that is not solid or a liquid.
گیس

gate *noun*
gates
A **gate** is a kind of door in a wall, a fence, or a hedge.
پھاٹک

gave
⇨ Look at **give**.
*She **gave** me a present.*

gentle *adjective*
gentler, gentlest
If you are **gentle**, you are careful and not rough.
شریف
*Be **gentle** when you hold the baby.*

get *verb*
gets, getting, got
1. You can use **get** to mean the same as "become".
   ہونا
   *We should go before it **gets** dark.*
2. If you **get** somewhere, you arrive there.
   پہنچنا
   *He **got** home at noon.*
3. If you **get** something, someone gives it to you.
   پانا، حاصل ہونا
   *I **got** a bike for my birthday.*
4. If you **get** something, you go to where it is and bring it back.
   لانا، حاصل کرنا
   *He went to **get** a cup of coffee.*

ghost *noun*
ghosts
A **ghost** is a dead person who some people think they can see and hear.
بھوت

giant *adjective*
Something that is **giant** is very large.
دیونما، دیو ہیکل، کافی بڑا
*They watched the film on a **giant** TV screen.*

giraffe *noun*
giraffes
A **giraffe** is a very tall animal with a long neck, long legs, and dark spots on its body.
جراف

girl *noun*
girls
A **girl** is a child or a young person who is a female.
لڑکی

give *verb*
gives, giving, gave, given
If you **give** someone something, you let them have it to keep.
دینا، دو
*We always **give** our mother flowers on her birthday.*

glad *adjective*
gladder, gladdest
If you are **glad**, you are happy about something.
خوش
*I'm **glad** you can come to my party.*

glass *noun*
glasses
1. **Glass** is a hard, clear material that is used to make things like windows and bottles. It is quite easy to break **glass**.
   شیشہ، بلور
   *The salad was in a **glass** bowl.*
2. A **glass** is also a container made from glass that you can drink out of.
   گلاس
   *He filled his **glass** with milk.*

glasses *noun*
Glasses are two pieces of plastic or glass in a frame that people wear in front of their eyes to help them to see better.
چشمہ

a b c d e f g h i j k l m n o p q r s t u v w x y z

glove *noun*
gloves
Gloves are things that you wear over your hands to keep them warm. **Gloves** have one part for your thumb and one for all your fingers.
دستانہ

glue *noun*
You use **glue** to stick things together.
گوند

go *verb*
goes, going, went, gone
1 If you **go** somewhere, you move there from another place.
جانا
*Can we **go** to the park?*
2 If you say that something is **going** to happen, you mean that it will happen.
جانا
*He's **going** to leave soon.*

goal *noun*
goals
In games like football, the **goal** is the place that you try to get the ball in to, to score a point.
گول، ہدف

goat *noun*
goats
A **goat** is an animal about the size of a sheep. **Goats** have horns, and hair on their chin that looks like a beard.
بکری

gold *noun*
Gold is a valuable, yellow metal that is used to make things like rings and necklaces, and also coins.
سونا

goldfish *noun*
goldfish
A **goldfish** is a small orange fish that people often keep as a pet.
نارنجی مچھلی

gone
⇨ Look at **go**.
*She has **gone** home.*

good *adjective*
better, best
1 If you say that something is **good**, you like it.
اچھا
*That was a **good** film.*
2 If you are **good**, you behave well.
اچھا
*Be **good** while I am out.*
3 If you are **good** at something, you do it well.
ماہر ہونا
*She is **good** at drawing.*

goodbye
You say **goodbye** to someone when one of you is going away.
خدا حافظ

good night
You say **good night** to someone late in the evening before you go home or go to bed.
شب بخیر

goose *noun*
geese
A **goose** is a large bird with a long neck that lives near water.
ہنس

gorilla *noun*
gorillas
A **gorilla** is a large, strong animal with long arms, black fur, and a black face.
گوریلا

got
⇨ Look at **get**.
*They soon **got** tired of the game.*

grain *noun*
grains
1 A **grain** is the seed of a cereal plant, for example rice or wheat.
اناج
2 A **grain** of something, for example sand or salt, is a tiny piece of it.
چھوٹا ٹکڑا

gram *noun*
grams
A **gram** is used for measuring how heavy things are.
گرام
*There are about 400 **grams** of jam in this jar.*

grandfather *noun*
grandfathers
Your **grandfather** is your father's father or your mother's father.
دادا، نانا

grandmother *noun*
grandmothers
Your **grandmother** is your father's mother or your mother's mother.
دادی، نانی

grape *noun*
grapes
A **grape** is a small, round, green or purple fruit that grows in bunches.
انگور

grapefruit *noun*
grapefruits
A **grapefruit** is a large, round, yellow fruit with a sour taste.
چکوترہ

graph *noun*
graphs
In maths, a **graph** is a picture that uses lines or shapes to show numbers.
گراف

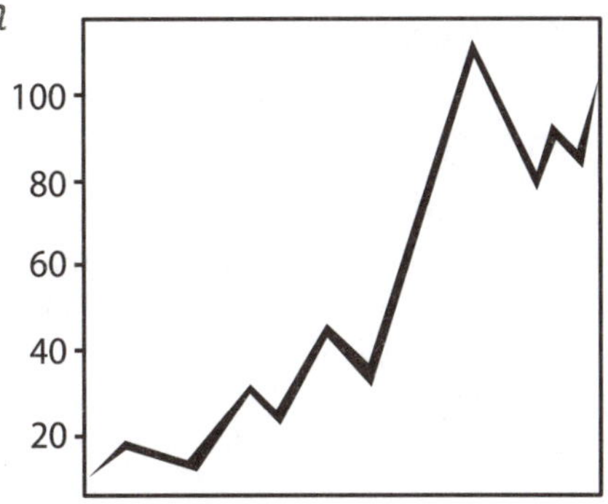

grass *noun*
grasses
Grass is a green plant with very thin leaves that cover the ground in fields and gardens.
گھاس

great *adjective*
greater, greatest
1 **Great** means very large.
عظیم، کافی بڑا، عظیم الشان
*The king lived in a **great** palace.*
2 **Great** also means very important.
عظیم، بہت بڑا/ بڑی
*The computer was a **great** invention.*
3 If you say that something is **great**, you mean that it is very good.
بہترین، بہت اچھا
*We had a **great** time.*

greedy *adjective*
greedier, greediest
If someone is **greedy**, they want to have more of something than they need.
لالچی
*He was so **greedy** that he ate the whole cake.*

green *noun*
Green is the colour of grass or leaves.
سبز، ہرا
*Her dress is **green**.*

grew
⇨ Look at **grow**.
*The tree **grew** to a great height.*

grey *noun*
Grey is a mixture of black and white, like the colour of clouds when rain is falling.
خاکستری رنگ

ground *noun*
The **ground** is the earth or other surface that you walk on outside.
سطح زمین

A B C D E F G H I J K L M N O P Q R S T U V W X Y Z

group *noun*
groups
A **group** is a number of people or things that are together, or that belong together.
گروہ

grow *verb*
grows, growing, grew, grown
When something **grows**, it gets bigger.
بڑھنا، نشونما پانا
*The puppy **grew** into a huge dog.*

guess *verb*
guesses, guessing, guessed
If you **guess**, you say what you think is true about something, but you do not really know if you are right.
اندازہ لگانا
*Can you **guess** how old he is?*

guinea pig *noun*
guinea pigs
A **guinea pig** is a small animal with fur and no tail that people often keep as a pet.
گنی پگ، ایک چھوٹا بغیر دم والا روئیں دار جاندار جسے لوگ پالتے ہیں۔

guitar *noun*
guitars
A **guitar** is an instrument with strings that you play by pressing the strings with one hand and pulling them with the other hand.
گٹار

Hh

had
⇨ Look at **have**.
*We **had** a nice time.*

hadn't
Hadn't is short for **had not**.
نہیں کرنا
*I **hadn't** seen them for a long time.*

hair *noun*
Hair is the soft, fine threads that grow on your head and on the bodies of many animals.
بال
*I wash my **hair** every night.*

half *noun*
halves
A **half** is one of two equal parts that make up a whole thing.
نصف، آدھا
*We each had **half** of the cake.*

halves
⇨ Look at **half**.
*Cut the apples into **halves**.*

hamster *noun*
hamsters
A **hamster** is a small animal that looks like a fat mouse with a short tail. People often keep **hamsters** as pets.
ہیمسٹر (چوہے جیسا بالدار جانور)

hand *noun*
hands
Your **hands** are the parts of your body that are at the ends of your arms, and that you use to hold things. A **hand** has four fingers and a thumb.
ہاتھ
*I put my **hand** in my pocket and took out the letter.*

handle *noun*
handles
1 A **handle** is something that is joined to a door, a window, or a drawer, that you use to open and close it.
ہینڈل، دستہ
*She pulled the **handle** of the drawer.*
2 A **handle** is also the part of something, for example a tool or a bag, that you use to hold it.
دستہ
*Hold the knife by its **handle**.*

hang *verb*
hangs, hanging, hung
If you **hang** something somewhere, you fix the top of it to something so that it does not touch the ground.
لٹکانا
*She **hung** her coat on a peg.*

happen *verb*
happens, happening, happened
When something **happens**, it takes place.
واقع ہونا، ہونا
*What's **happening** in the playground?*

happy *adjective*
happier, happiest
When you are **happy**, you feel pleased about something.
خوش

hard *adjective*
harder, hardest
1 Something that is **hard** is solid, and it is not easy to bend it or break it.
سخت
*The glass broke on the **hard** floor.*
2 If something is **hard**, you have to try a lot to do it or to understand it.
سخت، دشوار
*These sums are quite **hard**.*

has
⇨ Look at **have**.
*He **has** a sister.*

hasn't
Hasn't is short for **has not**.
نہیں کرنا
*She **hasn't** anything to do.*

hat *noun*
hats

A **hat** is something that you can wear on your head.
ٹوپ

hatch *verb*
hatches, hatching, hatched
When a baby bird or other animal **hatches**, it comes out of its egg by breaking the shell. You can also say that the egg **hatches**.
انڈے سینا

hate *verb*
hates, hating, hated
If you **hate** a person or a thing, you feel that you do not like them at all.
نفرت کرنا
*I **hate** onions.*

have *verb*
has, having, had
1 If you **have** something, it belongs to you.
رکھنا
*Do you **have** any pets?*
2 When you **have** something, you feel it, or it happens to you.
پاس ہونا
*I **have** a bad cold.*

a b c d e f g h i j k l m n o p q r s t u v w x y z

A B C D E F G H I J K L M N O P Q R S T U V W X Y Z

haven't

Haven't is short for **have not**.

پاس میں نہیں ہونا

*I **haven't** any chocolate left.*

hay *noun*

Hay is dry grass that is used to feed animals.

سوکھی گھاس

head *noun*

heads

1 Your **head** is the part of your body at the top that has your eyes, ears, nose, mouth, and brain in it.

سر

*The ball hit him on the **head**.*

2 The **head** of something is the person who is its leader.

سربراہ، صدر، قائد

*He is the **head** of the school.*

heal *verb*

heals, healing, healed

If something like a broken bone **heals**, it gets better.

مندمل ہونا

healthy *adjective*

healthier, healthiest

1 Someone who is **healthy** is well and strong and is not often ill.

صحت مند

*People need exercise to stay **healthy**.*

2 Something that is **healthy** is good for you.

صحت بخش

*Eat **healthy** food like fruit and vegetables.*

hear *verb*

hears, hearing, heard

When you **hear** a sound, you notice it through your ears.

سننا

*I **heard** a dog barking.*

heart *noun*

hearts

Your **heart** is the part inside you that makes the blood move around your body.

دل

*His **heart** was going fast.*

heavy *adjective*

heavier, heaviest

Something that is **heavy** weighs a lot.

بھاری

*This bag is very **heavy**.*

he'd

1 **He'd** is short for **he had**.

کرنا (ماضی)

***He'd** seen it before.*

2 **He'd** is also short for **he would**.

کرنا (مستقبل)

***He'd** like them.*

hedge *noun*

hedges

A **hedge** is a row of bushes growing close together that makes a kind of wall. You often see **hedges** around fields.

جھاڑی

heel *noun*

heels

Your **heels** are the parts of your feet at the back, below your ankles.

ایڑی

*He dragged his **heels** along the ground.*

height *noun*

heights

Your **height** is how tall you are.

قد

*We all measured our **heights**.*

held
⇨ Look at **hold**.
*Mum **held** my hand as we crossed the road.*

helicopter *noun*
helicopters
A **helicopter** is a small aircraft with long blades on top that go round very quickly. **Helicopters** can fly straight up and down and stay in one place in the air.
ہیلی کاپٹر

he'll
He'll is short for **he will**.
کرے گا
***He'll** come back soon.*

hello
You say **hello** to someone when you meet them.
ہلو!

help *verb*
helps, helping, helped
If you **help** someone, you make it easier for them to do something.
مدد
*He **helped** me with my homework.*

hen *noun*
hens
A **hen** is a chicken that is a female. People often eat **hens'** eggs as food.
مرغی

her
You use **her** to talk about a woman or a girl, or to say that something belongs to a woman or a girl.
اس کا (مؤنث)
*I gave **her** back **her** pen.*

herd *noun*
herds
A **herd** is a large group of animals that lives together.
جھنڈ، ریوڑ
*We saw a **herd** of deer in the forest.*

here
Here means the place where you are.
یہاں
*Come and sit **here**.*

hers
You use **hers** to say that something belongs to a woman or a girl.
اس کی (خاتون کی)
*She said that the bag was **hers**.*

herself
You use **herself** when you want to say that something a woman or a girl does has an effect on her.
وہ (خاتون) خود
*She pulled **herself** out of the water.*

he's
He's is short for **he is**.
ہونا
***He's** six years old.*

hexagon *noun*
hexagons
A **hexagon** is a shape with six straight sides.
ہشت پہلو

hid
⇨ Look at **hide**.
*They **hid** in the cupboard.*

A B C D E F G H I J K L M N O P Q R S T U V W X Y Z

hidden

⇨ Look at **hide**.

*He was **hidden** under the bed.*

hide *verb*

hides, hiding, hid, hidden

1 If you **hide** something, you put it where no one can see it or find it.

چھپانا

*He **hid** his bike behind the wall.*

2 If you **hide** what you feel, you do not let people know about it.

چھپانا، پردہ پوشی کرنا

*She tried to **hide** how angry she was.*

high *adjective*

higher, highest

1 Something that is **high** is tall or is a long way above the ground.

اونچا

*There was a **high** wall around the house.*

2 **High** also means great in amount or strength.

اونچا

*They charged us a **high** price.*

3 A **high** sound or voice goes up a long way.

بلند

*She spoke in a **high** voice.*

hill *noun*

hills

A **hill** is a piece of land that is higher than the land around it. **Hills** are not as high as mountains.

پہاڑی

him

You use **him** to talk about a man or a boy.

اس کو (مرد کو)

*We met **him** at the station.*

himself

You use **himself** when you want to say that something a man or a boy does has an effect on him.

وہ (مرد) خود

*He fell and hurt **himself**.*

hippopotamus *noun*

hippopotamuses or **hippopotami**

A **hippopotamus** is a large animal with short legs and thick skin that lives near rivers.

گینڈا

his

You use **his** to say that something belongs to a man or a boy.

اس کا

*He showed me **his** new football.*

history *noun*

History is the story of what has happened in the past.

تاریخ

hit *verb*

hits, hitting, hit

If you **hit** something, you touch it with a lot of strength.

مارنا، ٹھوکر لگانا

*She **hit** the ball with the bat.*

hive *noun*

hives

A **hive** is a place where bees live.

چھتہ

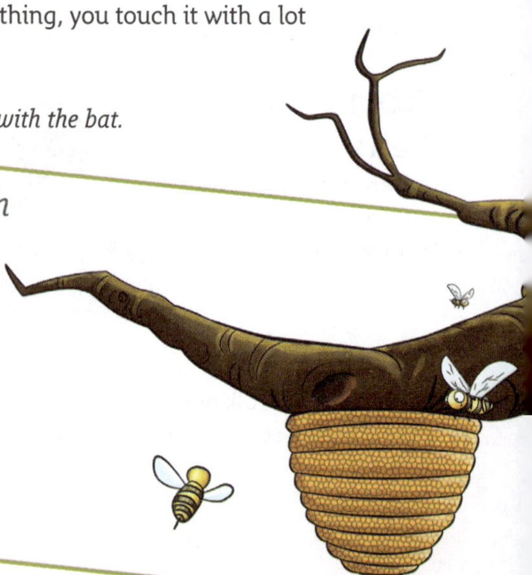

hold *verb*

holds, holding, held

1 When you **hold** something, you have it in your hands or your arms.

پکڑنا

*She **held** the baby in her arms.*

2 If something **holds** an amount of something, then that is how much it has room for inside.

گنجائش ہونا

*The theatre **holds** 400 people.*

hole *noun*

holes

A **hole** is a gap or a hollow place in something.

سوراخ

*We dug a **hole** in the ground.*

holiday *noun*

holidays

A **holiday** is a time when you do not need to work or go to school.

تعطیل، چھٹی کا دن

hollow *adjective*

Something that is **hollow** has an empty space inside it.

کھوکھلا

*The owl's nest was in a **hollow** tree.*

home *noun*

homes

Your **home** is the place where you live.

گھر کے طور پر

*We stayed at **home** and watched TV.*

homework *noun*

Homework is something like sums that a teacher gives you to work on at home.

گھر کا کام (ہوم ورک)

honest *adjective*

If someone is **honest**, they do not tell lies, and you can believe what they say.

ایماندار

honey *noun*

Honey is a sweet, very thick liquid that is made by bees. You can eat **honey** on bread.

شہد

hoof *noun*

hooves

A **hoof** is the hard part of a horse's foot. Deer and cows also have **hooves**.

کھر

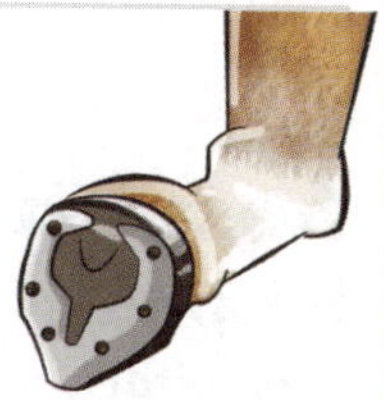

hop *verb*

hops, hopping, hopped

1 If you **hop**, you jump on one foot.

کودنا

2 When animals or birds **hop**, they jump with two feet together.

اچھلنا

hope *verb*

hopes, hoping, hoped

If you **hope** that something will happen, you want it to happen.

امید رکھنا، توقع کرنا

*I **hope** you feel better soon.*

horn *noun*

horns

1 A **horn** is one of the hard bones with sharp points that grow out of some animals' heads. Goats and bulls have **horns**.

سینگ

2 A **horn** is also an instrument that you blow into to make music.

ہارن

horrible *adjective*

If something is **horrible**, it is very nasty.

ڈراونا

*There was a **horrible** smell.*

a b c d e f g h i j k l m n o p q r s t u v w x y z

horse *noun*
horses
A **horse** is a large animal with a long tail and four legs. People ride on **horses** or use them to pull things along.
گھوڑا

hospital *noun*
hospitals
A **hospital** is a building where doctors and nurses care for people who are ill or hurt.
ہسپتال

hot *adjective*
hotter, hottest
If something is **hot**, it is very warm.
گرم
*Don't touch the plate – it's **hot**.*

hour *noun*
hours
An **hour** is used for measuring time. There are sixty minutes in an **hour**, and twenty-four **hours** in a day.
گھنٹہ

house *noun*
houses
A **house** is a building where people live.
گھر
*Come to my **house** for dinner.*

how
1 You use the word **how** when you ask about the way that something happens or the way that you do something.
کیسے، کس طرح
***How** do you spell your name?*
2 You also use **how** when you ask about an amount.
کتنے، کتنا
***How** many people were at the party?*

hug *verb*
hugs, hugging, hugged
When you **hug** someone, you put your arms around them and hold them close to you.
گلے لگانا، بغلگیر ہونا
*She **hugged** me as we said goodbye.*

huge *adjective*
Something that is **huge** is very big.
بڑی، دیو ہیکل
*Elephants are **huge** animals.*

human *adjective*
Something that is **human** is to do with people, and not animals or machines.
انسانی
*There are over 200 bones in the **human** body.*

hundred *noun*
A **hundred** is the number 100.
سو

hung
⇨ Look at **hang**.
*He **hung** from the bars.*

hungry *adjective*
hungrier, hungriest
If you are **hungry**, you want to eat something.
بھوکا

hunt *verb*
hunts, hunting, hunted
1 When animals **hunt**, they chase another animal to kill it for food.
شکار کرنا
*The lions **hunted** a zebra.*
2 If you **hunt** for something, you try to find it.
تلاش کرنا
*I **hunted** for my keys.*

hurry *verb*
hurries, hurrying, hurried
If you **hurry**, you move quickly or do something quickly.
جلدی میں ہونا
*We'll be late if we don't **hurry**.*

hurt *verb*
hurts, hurting, hurt
If you **hurt** someone or something, you make them feel pain.
چوٹ پہنچانا
*I fell over and **hurt** my leg yesterday.*

husband *noun*
husbands
A woman's **husband** is the man she is married to.
شوہر

hut *noun*
huts
A **hut** is a small building with one or two rooms. **Huts** are made of wood, mud, or grass.
جھونپڑی

hutch *noun*
hutches
A **hutch** is a kind of cage made of wood and wire, where people keep rabbits and other small pets.
پنجرہ

Ii

I
You use **I** to talk about yourself.
میں
***I** like chocolate.*

ice *noun*
Ice is water that has frozen. It is very cold and hard.
برف
*The ground was covered with **ice**.*

ice cream *noun*
Ice cream is a very cold, sweet food that is made from frozen milk or cream.
آئس کریم

icicle *noun*
icicles
An **icicle** is a long piece of ice with a point at the end that hangs down from something. **Icicles** are made from dripping water that has frozen.
برف کا قلم، جو غاروں کی چھت سے ٹپکتے پانی کے منجمد ہونے پر بن جاتا ہے۔

I'd
1 **I'd** is short for **I had**.
کیا (ماضی)
***I'd** been there before.*
2 **I'd** is also short for **I would**.
کروں گا (مستقبل)
***I'd** like to go to the zoo.*

idea *noun*
ideas

An **idea** is something new that you have thought of.

خیال

*He had an **idea** for a story.*

ill *adjective*

When you are **ill**, you do not feel well.

بیمار

*She is too **ill** to go to school.*

I'll

I'll is short for **I will**.

کروں گا (مستقبل)

***I'll** come back tomorrow.*

illness *noun*
illnesses

If you have an **illness**, you do not feel well.

بیماری

*He has just had a very bad **illness**.*

I'm

I'm is short for **I am**.

میں ہوں

***I'm** hungry.*

imagine *verb*
imagines, imagining, imagined

If you **imagine** something, you make a picture of it in your mind.

خیال کرنا، تصور کرنا

***Imagine** that you are a cat.*

immediately

If you do something **immediately**, you do it now.

فوری طور پر

*Stop that noise **immediately**!*

important *adjective*

1 If something is **important**, people care about it and think about it a lot.

اہم، ضروری

*It is **important** not to tell lies.*

2 If someone is **important**, people pay a lot of attention to what they say and do.

اہم

*She is a very **important** person.*

impossible *adjective*

If something is **impossible**, it cannot be done, or it cannot happen.

ناممکن

*It is **impossible** to see in the dark.*

in

1 **In** means not outside.

اندر

*The juice is **in** the fridge.*

2 You also use **in** to say when something happens.

میں

*He was born **in** March.*

inch *noun*
inches

An **inch** is used for measuring the length of something. There are about two and half centimetres in an **inch**.

انچ

indoors

If you are **indoors**, you are inside a building.

اندرونی طور پر

information *noun*

Information about something is facts that tell you about it.

معلومات

*I need some **information** about birds.*

ink *noun*
Ink is a liquid that you use to write or print with. Pens have **ink** inside them.
روشنائی

insect *noun*
insects
An **insect** is a small animal with six legs, for example a bee or a beetle. Many **insects** have wings and can fly.
کیڑا، حشرہ

inside
1 If something is **inside** another thing, it is in it.
اندر
*There was a letter **inside** the envelope.*
2 **Inside** also means indoors.
گھر کے اندر
*He went **inside** and locked the door.*

instructions *noun*
Instructions are words or pictures that tell you how to do something.
ہدایات
*Here are the **instructions** for building the tent.*

instrument *noun*
instruments
1 An **instrument** is a tool that you use to do something.
آلہ، اوزار
*The doctor used an **instrument** to look in my ears.*
2 An **instrument** is also something, for example a piano or a guitar, that you use to make music.
آلہ موسیقی
*He plays three **instruments**.*

intelligent *adjective*
If a person is **intelligent**, they are able to understand and learn things quickly.
عاقل

interesting *adjective*
If something is **interesting**, you want to know more about it.
دلچسپ

Internet *noun*
The **Internet** is something that joins a computer to other computers all over the world. You send emails using the **Internet**.
انٹرنیٹ

interrupt *verb*
interrupts, interrupting, interrupted
If you **interrupt** someone, you say or do something that makes them stop in the middle of what they are doing.
رکاوٹ ڈالنا
*Don't **interrupt** the teacher when she's talking.*

invention *noun*
inventions
An **invention** is something that someone has made, and that nobody has ever thought of or made before.
ایجاد
*His new **invention** is a car that can fly.*

invisible *adjective*
If something is **invisible**, you cannot see it.
نادیدہ

invite *verb*
invites, inviting, invited
If you **invite** someone to something, for example a party, you ask them to come to it.
دعوت دینا

a b c d e f g h i j k l m n o p q r s t u v w x y z

iron *noun*
irons

1 **Iron** is a strong, hard, grey metal.
لوہا، فولاد

2 An **iron** is a piece of equipment with a flat bottom that gets hot. You move the bottom over clothes to make them smooth.
استری

is
⇨ Look at **be**.
*She **is** six years old.*

island *noun*
islands
An **island** is a piece of land that has water all around it.
جزیرہ

isn't
Isn't is short for **is not**.
نہیں ہے
*He **isn't** very happy.*

it
You use **it** to talk about a thing or an animal.
یہ (بے جان کے لئے)
*This is a good book – have you read **it**?*

its
You use **its** to say that something belongs to a thing or an animal.
اس کا
*The lion lifted **its** head.*

it's
It's is short for **it is**.
یہ ہے
***It's** one o'clock.*

I've
I've is short for **I have**.
میں نے
***I've** been playing football.*

Jj

jacket *noun*
jackets
A **jacket** is a short coat.
جیکیٹ

jam *noun*
Jam is a soft, sweet food that is made from fruit and sugar.
جام (بریڈ والا)
*I love strawberry **jam** on my bread.*

January *noun*
January is the month after December and before February. It has 31 days.
جنوری

jar *noun*
jars
A **jar** is a glass container with a lid that is used for storing food.
مرتبان
*Make sure you put the lid back on the **jar**.*

jaw *noun*
jaws
Your **jaws** are the top and bottom bones of your mouth.
جبڑا

jeans *noun*
Jeans are blue trousers with pockets at the front and back.
جینس (پتلون)
*Everyone on the trip wore **jeans** and a bright T-shirt.*

jelly *noun*
Jelly is a clear, sweet food that is solid but soft.
جیلی (شفاف مٹھائی)
*We had birthday cake, then **jelly** and ice cream.*

jet *noun*
jets
A **jet** is a plane that flies very fast.
جیٹ (ہوائی جہاز)

jewel *noun*
jewels
1 A **jewel** is a valuable stone, like a diamond.
نگینہ، جڑاؤ پتھر
2 **Jewels** are things made with valuable stones, that you wear to decorate your body.
زیور
*She put the **jewels** in the box and turned the key.*

jigsaw *noun*
jigsaws
A **jigsaw** is a picture on cardboard that has been cut up into pieces. You have to fit them together again.
آڑاکٹا معا (تصویر کے ٹکڑے۔جوڑنا)
*The children put the last pieces in the **jigsaw**.*

job *noun*
jobs
A **job** is the work that a person does to earn money.
کام (روزگار)
*My sister wants to get a **job**.*

join *verb*
joins, joining, joined
1 If you **join** a group of people, you become one of the group.
شامل ہونا
*Come and **join** the music group after school on Mondays.*
2 When things **join**, or you **join** them, they come together.
جوڑنا، ملانا
*They **joined** hands and danced.*

joke *noun*
jokes
A **joke** is something that someone says to make you laugh.
لطیفہ
*Grandfather always tells us **jokes** after dinner.*

journey *noun*
journeys
When you make a **journey**, you travel from one place to another.
سفر
*It was a difficult **journey** that took several days.*

jug *noun*
jugs
A **jug** is a container with a handle. You use a **jug** for pouring liquids.
جگ
*There is a **jug** of cold water on the table.*

juice *noun*
juices
Juice is the liquid from a fruit or vegetable.
رس، جوس
*He had a large glass of fresh orange **juice**.*

July *noun*
July is the month after June and before August.
It has 31 days.
جولائی

jump *verb*
jumps, jumping, jumped
When you **jump**, you bend your knees and push yourself into the air.
جست لگانا، کودنا
*I **jumped** over the fence.*

jumper *noun*
jumpers
You wear a **jumper** to keep yourself warm. It has sleeves and covers the top half of your body.
جمپر

June *noun*
June is the month after May and before July.
It has 30 days.
جون

jungle *noun*
jungles
A **jungle** is a thick, wet forest in a hot country.
جنگل
*They followed the path deep into the **jungle**.*

just
If you **just** did something, you did it a very short time ago.
بس ابھی، ٹھیک
*We **just** got home after an awful journey.*

Kk

kangaroo *noun*
kangaroos
A **kangaroo** is a large Australian animal that carries its babies in a pocket on its stomach.
کنگارو

keen *adjective*
keener, keenest
If you are **keen**, you want to do something very much.
شائق
*Everyone was **keen** to help.*

keep *verb*
keeps, keeping, kept
1 If someone **keeps** away from a place, they do not go near it.
رکھنا
__Keep__ away from the road.
2 If someone **keeps** still or warm, they stay like that.
رکھنا
*We lit a fire to **keep** warm.*
*"**Keep** still!"*
3 If you **keep** doing something, you do it many times or you do it some more.
جاری رکھنا، برقرار رکھنا
*I **keep** forgetting to take my umbrella.*
4 When you **keep** something, you store it somewhere.
حفاظت سے رکھنا
*She **kept** her money under the bed.*

kennel *noun*
kennels
A **kennel** is a small house where a dog can sleep.
کتا گھر

kept
⇨ Look at **keep**.
*She **kept** her head down.*

kettle *noun*
kettles

A **kettle** is a metal container with a lid and a handle, that you use for boiling water.

کیتلی

*Mum put the **kettle** on and made some tea.*

key *noun*
keys

1. A **key** is a piece of metal that opens or closes a lock.
   چابی، کنجی
   *They put the **key** in the door and it opened.*
2. The **keys** on a computer or instrument are the buttons that you press on it.
   کلید، کمپیوٹر وغیرہ کے کی بورڈ پر موجود کلیدیں
   *Press the "Enter" **key**.*

kick *verb*
kicks, kicking, kicked

If you **kick** something, you hit it with your foot.

ٹھوکر مارنا

*He **kicked** the ball really hard.*

kid *noun*
kids

A **kid** is a child.

بچہ

*They have three **kids**.*

kill *verb*
kills, killing, killed

To **kill** a living thing is to make it die.

مارنا، قتل کرنا

*The earthquake **killed** 62 people.*

kilogram *noun*
kilograms

A **kilogram** is used for measuring how heavy things are. There are 1,000 grams in a **kilogram**.

کلوگرام

*The box weighs 4.5 **kilograms**.*

kilometre *noun*
kilometres

A **kilometre** is used for measuring distance. There are 1,000 metres in a **kilometre**, which is about 0.62 miles.

کلو میٹر

kind *noun*
kinds

A **kind** of thing is a type or sort of that thing.

قسم

*What **kind** of car is that?*

kind *adjective*
kinder, kindest

Someone who is **kind** is friendly and helps you.

مہربان، رحم دل

*Thank you for being so **kind** to me.*

king *noun*
kings

A **king** is a man who rules a country.

بادشاہ

*We saw the **king** and queen arriving.*

kiss *verb*
kisses, kissing, kissed

If you **kiss** someone, you touch them with your lips.

بوسہ لینا

*We **kissed** goodbye at the airport.*

kitchen *noun*
kitchens

A **kitchen** is a room that is used for cooking.

باورچی خانہ

kite *noun*

kites

A **kite** is a toy that you fly in the wind at the end of a long string.

پتنگ

*We went to the beach to fly **kites**.*

kitten *noun*

kittens

A **kitten** is a very young cat.

بلی کا بچہ

knee *noun*

knees

Your **knee** is the part in the middle of your leg where it bends.

گھٹنا

*I fell over and hurt my **knee**.*

kneel *verb*

kneels, kneeling, knelt

When you **kneel**, you bend your legs and rest on one or both of your knees.

دوزانو ہونا

*She **knelt** down beside the bed.*

knew

➾ Look at **know**.

*I **knew** all the kids at the party.*

knife *noun*

knives

A **knife** is a sharp metal tool that you use to cut things.

چاقو، چھری

*I finished and put down my **knife** and fork.*

knight *noun*

knights

In the past, a **knight** was a soldier who rode a horse.

شہ سوار

knit *verb*

knits, knitting, knitted

If you **knit** something, you make it from a long piece of wool by using two special sticks.

بننا

*My grandmother sat **knitting**.*

knives

➾ Look at **knife**.

*We put all the **knives** away in their box.*

knock *verb*

knocks, knocking, knocked

If you **knock** on something, you hit it to make a noise.

کھٹکھٹانا

*She went to his house and **knocked** on the door.*

knot *noun*

knots

You make a **knot** when you tie two pieces of something together.

گرہ، گانٹھ

*He picked up the rope and tied a **knot** in it.*

know *verb*

knows, knowing, knew, known

1 If you **know** something, you have that information in your mind.

جاننا، معلوم ہونا

*You should **know** the answer to that question.*

2 If you **know** a person, you have met them and spoken to them.

جاننا

*I didn't **know** any of the other people in the class.*

Ll

label *noun*
labels

A **label** is a small note on something that gives you information about it.

لیبل

*The prices are on the **labels**.*

lace *noun*
laces

1 **Lace** is a pretty cloth that has patterns of holes in it.

لیس، زریں چمکدار پٹی

*Her dress was dark blue with a white **lace** collar.*

2 **Laces** are like pieces of string for fastening shoes.

فیتہ

*He put on his shoes and tied the **laces**.*

ladder *noun*
ladders

A **ladder** is a set of steps that you can move around. You use it for reaching high places.

سیڑھی

*He climbed the **ladder** to see over the wall.*

lady *noun*
ladies

You can use **lady** to talk about a woman in a polite way.

خاتون

*She's a very nice old **lady**.*

ladybird *noun*
ladybirds

A **ladybird** is a small round beetle that has red wings with black spots.

سیاہ چتی والا بادامی بھونرا

laid
⇨ Look at **lay**.

*She **laid** out the food on the table.*

lain
⇨ Look at **lie**.

*He had **lain** awake all night, worrying.*

lake *noun*
lakes

A **lake** is an area of water with land around it.

جھیل

lamb *noun*
lambs

A **lamb** is a young sheep.

بھیڑ کا بچہ

lamp *noun*
lamps

A **lamp** is a light that uses electricity, oil or gas.

چراغ، بلب

*She turned on the **lamp** by her bed.*

land *noun*
Land is an area of ground.

زمین

*This is good farm **land**.*

land *verb*
lands, landing, landed

When something **lands**, it comes down to the ground after moving through the air.

اترنا

*The ball **landed** in the middle of the road.*

lane *noun*
lanes

A **lane** is a narrow road, usually in the country.

گلی

a b c d e f g h i j k l m n o p q r s t u v w x y z

language *noun*
languages

A **language** is a set of words that the people of a country use in talking or writing.

زبان

*The English **language** has over 500,000 words.*

lap *noun*
laps

Your **lap** is the flat area on top of your thighs when you are sitting down.

گود

*The boy sat on his dad's **lap**.*

large *adjective*
larger, largest

A **large** thing or person is big or bigger than usual.

بڑا، جسیم

*This fish lives in **large** rivers and lakes.*

last *adjective*

1. The **last** thing is the one before this one.
   آخری
   *In the **last** lesson, we looked at some flowers.*
2. The **last** thing or person comes after all the others.
   آخری، اختتامی
   *I read the **last** three pages of the chapter.*

late
later, latest

1. **Late** means near the end of a period of time.
   دیر
   *It was **late** in the afternoon.*
2. **Late** also means after the proper time.
   تاخیر سے
   *We arrived **late** for our class.*

laugh *verb*
laughs, laughing, laughed

When you **laugh**, you smile and make a sound because something is funny.

ہنسنا

*The boys all **laughed** at his joke.*

law *noun*
laws

A **law** is a rule that tells people what they may or may not do in a country.

قانون

lawn *noun*
lawns

A **lawn** is an area of short grass.

گھاس کا میدان

*Let's sit on the **lawn**.*

lay *verb*
lays, laying, laid

1. When you **lay** something somewhere, you put it down so that it lies there.
   رکھنا، پھیلانا
   ***Lay** the dishes on the table.*
2. When a bird **lays** an egg, it pushes an egg out of its body.
   دینا

lay

⇨ Look at **lie**.

*We **lay** on the grass and looked at the sky.*

layer *noun*
layers

A **layer** is something that covers a surface, or that lies between two other things.

پرت

*A **layer** of new snow covered the street.*

lazy *adjective*
lazier, laziest

A **lazy** person does not like working.

سست

*He was too **lazy** to read the whole book.*

lead *verb*
leads, leading, led

If you **lead** someone to a place, you take them there.

رہنمائی کرنا

*I took his hand and started to **lead** him into the house.*

lead *noun*

If you are in the **lead** in a race or competition, you are winning.

آگے ہونا، بڑھت حاصل کرنا

*Our team was in the **lead** after ten minutes.*

lead *noun*

Lead is a soft, grey, heavy metal.

سیسہ

leader *noun*

leaders

The **leader** of a group of people or a country is the person who is in charge of it.

رہنما

*Your team **leaders** have your instructions.*

leaf *noun*

leaves

The **leaves** of a plant are the parts that are flat, thin, and usually green.

پتہ، پتی

*A dry, brown **leaf** floated on the water.*

lean *verb*

leans, leaning, leant or **leaned**

When you **lean**, you bend your body from your waist.

جھکنا

*She **leant** forwards and looked at me again.*

leap *verb*

leaps, leaping, leapt or **leaped**

If you **leap**, you jump a long way or very high.

اچھلنا، جست لگانا

*He **leaped** in the air and waved his hands.*

learn *verb*

learns, learning, learnt or **learned**

When you **learn** something, you get to know it or how to do it.

سیکھنا، علم حاصل کرنا

*When did you **learn** to swim?*

leather *noun*

Leather is the skin of some animals that you can use for making things.

چمڑا

*Is your jacket made of real **leather**?*

leave *verb*

leaves, leaving, left

1 When you **leave** a place, you go away from it.

روانہ ہونا، روانگی

*Our bus **leaves** in an hour.*

2 If you **leave** something somewhere, you do not bring it with you.

چھوڑنا

*I **left** my bags in the car.*

leaves

⇨ Look at **leaf**.

*The **leaves** are beginning to turn brown.*

led

⇨ Look at **lead**.

*The woman **led** me through the door into her office.*

left *noun*

The **left** is one side of something. For example, on a page, English writing begins on the **left**.

بائیں

*The school is on the **left** at the end of the road.*

left

⇨ Look at **leave**.

*The teacher suddenly **left** the room.*

leg *noun*
legs

1 A person's or animal's **legs** are the long parts of their body that they use for walking and standing.
ٹانگ
*Stand with your arms stretched out and your **legs** apart.*

2 The **legs** of a table or chair are the long parts that it stands on.
پائنچہ
*One of the **legs** is loose.*

lemon *noun*
lemons

A **lemon** is a yellow fruit with very sour juice.
لیموں

lend *verb*
lends, lending, lent

If you **lend** someone something, you give it to them for a period of time and then they give it back to you.
قرض دینا، ادھار دینا، مستعار دینا
*Will you **lend** me your pen?*

length *noun*
lengths

The **length** of something is how long it is from one end to the other.
لمبائی
*The table is about a metre in **length**.*

lent

⇨ Look at **lend**.
*I **lent** her two books to read on holiday.*

leopard *noun*
leopards

A **leopard** is a large, wild cat. **Leopards** have yellow fur with black spots, and live in Africa and Asia.
چیتا، تیندوا

less *adjective*

Less means a smaller amount.
کم، تھوڑا
*I am trying to spend **less** money on sweets.*

lesson *noun*
lessons

A **lesson** is a period of time when someone teaches you something.
سبق
*My sister has a piano **lesson** every Monday.*

let *verb*
lets, letting, let

1 If you **let** someone do something, you allow them to do it.
اجازت دینا

2 You can say **let's** when you want someone to do something with you. **Let's** is short for **let us**.
شروع کرنا
***Let's** go!*

letter *noun*
letters

1 A **letter** is a message on paper that you post to someone.
خط
*I received a **letter** from a friend.*

2 **Letters** are shapes that you write to make words.
حروف تہجی
*The children practised writing the **letters** in class.*

lettuce *noun*
lettuces

A **lettuce** is a vegetable with large green leaves that you eat in salads.
کاہو، سلاد

library *noun*
libraries

A **library** is a place where you can go to read or borrow books.
لائبریری
*I'm going to the **library** to look for a book about whales.*

lick *verb*
licks, licking, licked

If you **lick** something, you move your tongue over it.
چاٹنا
***Lick** the stamp before you put it on the envelope.*

A B C D E F G H I J K L M N O P Q R S T U V W X Y Z

lid *noun*
lids
A **lid** is the top of a container that you can remove.
ڈھکن
*She lifted the **lid** of the box.*

lie *verb*
lies, lying, lay, lain
When you **lie** somewhere, your body is flat, and you are not standing or sitting.
لیٹنا
***Lie** on the bed and close your eyes for a while.*

lie *noun*
lies
A **lie** is something you say that is not true.
جھوٹ بولنا
*You told me a **lie**!*

life *noun*
lives
Your **life** is the period of time when you are alive.
زِندگی
*I want to live here for the rest of my **life**.*

lift *verb*
lifts, lifting, lifted
When you **lift** something, you take it and move it up.
اٹھانا
*He **lifted** the bag on to his shoulder.*

light *noun*
lights
1 **Light** is the bright energy that comes from the sun, that lets you see things.
روشنی
*A little **light** comes into the room through the thin curtains.*
2 A **light** is something like a lamp, that allows you to see.
روشنی
*There was only one small **light** in the room.*

light *adjective*
lighter, lightest
1 If a place is **light**, it is bright because of the sun or lamps.
روشن ہونا
*It gets **light** at about 6 o'clock here.*
2 Something that is **light** is not heavy.
ہلکا/ ہلکی ہونا
*The chair is quite **light** so we can move it if we want to.*
3 A **light** colour is pale.
ہلکا/ ہلکی
*His shirt was **light** blue.*

light *verb*
lights, lighting, lit
When you **light** a fire, it starts burning.
جلانا
*We used a whole box of matches to **light** the fire.*

lightning *noun*
Lightning is the very bright flashes of light in the sky in a storm.
بجلی
*There was thunder and **lightning** and big black clouds in the sky.*

like
1 If things or people are **like** each other, they are almost the same.
پسند کرنا
*He's very funny, **like** my uncle.*
2 You say what something or someone is **like** when you are talking about how they seem to you.
جیسا ہونا
*"What was the party **like**?"—"Oh it was great!"*

like *verb*
likes, liking, liked
If you **like** something, you think it is nice or interesting.
پسند کرنا
*Do you **like** swimming?*

A B C D E F G H I J K L M N O P Q R S T U V W X Y Z

line *noun*
lines
A **line** is a long, thin mark or shape.
خط
*Draw a **line** at the bottom of the page.*

lion *noun*
lions
A **lion** is a large wild cat that lives in Africa. **Lions** have yellow fur, and male **lions** have long hair on their head and neck.
شیر

lip *noun*
lips
Your **lips** are the edges of your mouth.
ہونٹ
*He bit his **lip**.*

liquid *noun*
liquids
A **liquid** is something that you can pour. Water and oil are **liquids**.
سیال
*The bottle is full of clear **liquid**.*

list *noun*
lists
A **list** is a set of names or other things that you write one below the other.
فہرست
*There are six names on the **list**.*

listen *verb*
listens, listening, listened
If you **listen** to something, you hear it and give it your attention.
سننا
*He's **listening** to the radio.*

lit
⇨ Look at **light**.
*He took a match and **lit** the candle.*

litre *noun*
litres
A **litre** is used for measuring liquid.
لیٹر

litter *noun*
Litter is rubbish that people drop in the street.
کوڑا کرکٹ
*Please don't drop any **litter**.*

little *adjective*
littler, littlest
A person or thing that is **little** is small in size.
چھوٹا، چھوٹی
*They live in a **little** house.*

live *verb*
lives, living, lived
1 You **live** in the place where your home is.
رہنا
*Where do you **live**?*
2 To **live** means to be alive.
زندہ رہنا
*We all need water to **live**.*

lives
⇨ Look at **life**.
*Their **lives** were changed.*

lizard *noun*
lizards
A **lizard** is a small reptile with a long tail and rough skin.
چھپکلی

load *verb*
loads, loading, loaded
If you **load** a vehicle, you put something on it.
بار کرنا، لادنا
*We finished **loading** the bags on to the lorry.*

loaf *noun*
loaves

A **loaf** is bread that you cut into slices.

ڈبل روٹی

*He bought a **loaf** of bread and some cheese.*

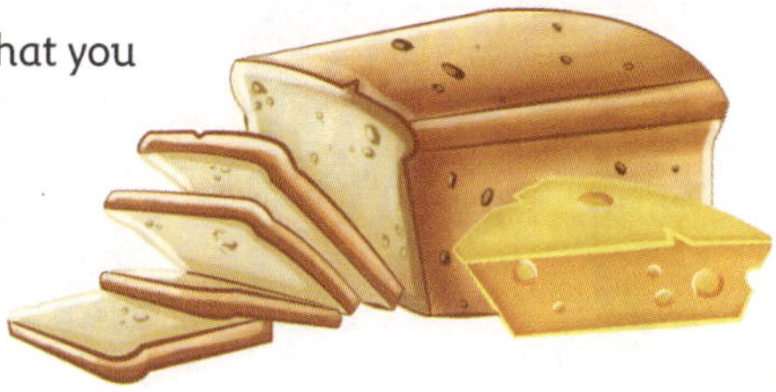

lock *verb*
locks, locking, locked

When you **lock** a door, you close it with a key.

مقفل کرنا

*Are you sure you **locked** the front door?*

log *noun*
logs

A **log** is a thick piece of wood from a tree.

لٹھا

*We sat around a **log** fire.*

lolly *noun*
lollies

A **lolly** is a sweet or ice cream on a stick.

لالی پوپ

long *adjective*
longer, longest

1 Something that is **long** takes a lot of time.

طویل، لمبا

*The afternoon lessons seemed very **long**.*

2 Something that is **long** measures a great distance from one end to the other.

طویل، لمبا

*There is a **long** table in the middle of the kitchen.*

look *verb*
looks, looking, looked

1 When you **look** at something, you turn your eyes so that you can see it.

دیکھنا

*I **looked** at the clock and yawned.*

2 You use **look** when you describe how a person seems.

نظر آنا

*The little girl **looked** sad.*

loose *adjective*
looser, loosest

1 Something that is **loose** moves when it should not.

ڈھیلا

*One of the table legs is **loose**.*

2 **Loose** clothes are rather large and are not tight.

ڈھیلا ڈھالا

*Wear **loose**, comfortable clothes when you do the exercises.*

lorry *noun*
lorries

A **lorry** is a large vehicle for moving things by road.

لاری، ٹرک

lose *verb*
loses, losing, lost

1 If you **lose** a game, you do not win it.

ہار جانا

*Our team **lost** the match by one point.*

2 If you **lose** something, you do not know where it is.

کھونا

*I've **lost** my keys.*

lost *adjective*

If you are **lost**, you do not know where you are.

کھویا ہوا

*I suddenly knew that I was **lost**.*

lot or lots

A **lot** of something, or **lots** of something, is a large amount of it.

کافی، بہت زیادہ

*He drank **lots** of milk.*

loud *adjective*
louder, loudest

A **loud** noise is a very big sound.

تیز آواز، شور

*The music was very **loud**.*

love *verb*
loves, loving, loved

1. If you **love** someone, you care very much about them.
   پیار کرنا، محبت کرنا خیال رکھنا
2. If you **love** something, you like it very much.
   محبت کرنا، پیار کرنا
   *We both **love** football.*

lovely *adjective*
lovelier, loveliest

A **lovely** thing or person is very beautiful or very nice.
پیارا
*I thought she looked **lovely**.*

low *adjective*
lower, lowest

1. Something that is **low** is close to the ground.
   نیچے / پست ہونا
   *There is a **low** fence around the house.*
2. A **low** number is a small number.
   چھوٹا، کمتر، کم
   *The price was very **low**.*

lucky *adjective*
luckier, luckiest

Someone who is **lucky** enjoys good things that people don't expect to happen.
قسمت والا
*He was **lucky** to win the competition.*

lump *noun*
lumps

A **lump** is a solid piece of something.
ڈھیر، ڈھیلا
*There was a bowl full of **lumps** of sugar.*

lunch *noun*
lunches

Lunch is the meal that you have in the middle of the day.
دوپہر کا کھانا (ظہرانہ)

lying

⇨ Look at **lie**.
*There was a man **lying** on the ground.*

Mm

machine *noun*
machines

A **machine** is a piece of equipment that uses electricity or an engine to do something.
مشین
*I left a message on the answering **machine**.*

made

⇨ Look at **make**.
*Mum **made** me a big birthday cake.*

magazine *noun*
magazines

A **magazine** is a thin book with stories and pictures in it.
رسالہ
*I get my favourite **magazine** every Thursday.*

magic *noun*

In stories, **magic** is a special power that allows you to do impossible things.
جادو
*By **magic**, the man turned to stone.*

magnet *noun*
magnets

A **magnet** is a piece of metal that attracts iron towards it.
مقناطیس

main *adjective*

The **main** thing is the most important one.

خاص، اہم

*That's the **main** reason I want it.*

make *verb*

makes, making, made

1 If you **make** something, you put it together or build it from other things.

بنانا

*She **makes** all her own clothes.*

2 You can use **make** to show that a person does or says something.

کرنا

*He **made** a phone call.*

3 If you **make** a person do something, they must do it.

کہنا، مجبور کرنا

*Mum **made** me clean the bathroom.*

male *adjective*

A **male** person or animal could become a father.

مرد، مذکر

*All of the pupils were **male**.*

mammal *noun*

mammals

Mammals are animals that feed their babies with milk.

پستان دار جانور (پستان سے دودھ پلانے والے)

*Some **mammals**, like whales, live in the sea.*

man *noun*

men

A **man** is an adult male person.

آدمی

*The book is for both **men** and women.*

manage *verb*

manages, managing, managed

If you **manage** something, you control it.

انتظام کرنا

*He **managed** the bank for 20 years.*

many *adjective*

If there are **many** people or things, there are a lot of them.

بہت سارے

*Does he have **many** friends?*

map *noun*

maps

A **map** is a drawing of an area from above. It shows where the roads, rivers and railways are.

نقشہ

*You can see the park beside this road on the **map**.*

March *noun*

March is the month after February and before April. It has 31 days.

مارچ

mark *noun*

marks

1 A **mark** is a small dirty area on a surface.

دھبہ

*I can't get this **mark** off my shirt.*

2 A **mark** is a shape that you write or draw.

نشان

*He made a few **marks** with his pen.*

market *noun*

markets

A **market** is a place where people buy and sell things.

بازار

*There's a **market** in the town centre every Saturday morning.*

marmalade *noun*

Marmalade is jam that is made from oranges.

نارنگی کا مربہ

marry *verb*

marries, marrying, married

When a man and a woman **marry**, they become husband and wife.

شادی کرنا

mask *noun*

masks

A **mask** is something that you wear over your face to protect or hide it.

نقاب، مکھوٹا

a b c d e f g h i j k l m n o p q r s t u v w x y z

mat *noun*
mats

A **mat** is a small piece of cloth, wood, or plastic that you put on a table to protect it.
چٹائی
*I put my glass on a red **mat**.*

match *noun*
matches

1 A **match** is a small, thin stick that makes a flame when you rub it on a rough surface.
ماچس کی تیلی
*She lit a **match** and held it up to the candle.*

2 A **match** is a game of football, cricket, or some other sport.
مقابلہ، میچ
*We won all our **matches** last year.*

match *verb*
matches, matching, matched

If one thing **matches** another, they look good together.
مماثل ہونا
*Do these shoes **match** my dress?*

material *noun*
materials

1 **Material** is cloth.
مادہ، میٹریل
*Her skirt was made from thick black **material**.*

2 A **material** is what something is made of, like rock, glass or plastic.
مادہ
*Wax is a soft **material**.*

maths *noun*

If you learn **maths**, you learn about numbers, shapes, and amounts.
ریاضی

matter *verb*
matters, mattered

If something **matters** to you, it is important.
اہمیت ہونا
*Never mind, it doesn't **matter**.*

may *verb*

1 If you **may** do something, it is possible that you will do it.
سکنا
*I **may** come back next year.*

2 If you **may** do something, you can do it because someone allows you to do it.
سکنا
*Please **may** I leave the room?*

May *noun*

May is the month after April and before June. It has 31 days.
مئی

me

You use **me** when you are talking about yourself.
مجھے
*Can you hear **me**?*

meal *noun*
meals

A **meal** is food that you eat at one time. Breakfast, lunch and dinner are **meals**.
کھانا
*She sat next to me for every **meal**.*

mean *verb*
means, meaning, meant

1 If you ask what something **means**, you want to understand it.
معنی، مفہوم
*What does this word **mean**?*

2 If you **mean** what you are saying, it is not a joke.
مطلب ہونا
*He says he loves her, and I think he **means** it.*

3 If you **mean** to do something, it is not an accident.
مقصد ہونا
*I didn't **mean** to drop the cup.*

mean *adjective*
meaner, meanest

Someone who is **mean** is not nice to other people.
ایذا پہنچانا، نفرت کرنا
*He was sorry for being **mean** to her.*

measles *noun*
Measles is an illness that gives you a fever and red spots on your skin.
خسرہ

measure *verb*
measures, measuring, measured
If you **measure** something, you find its size.
ناپنا، پیمائش کرنا
*First **measure** the length of the table.*

meat *noun*
Meat is the part of an animal that people cook and eat.
گوشت
*I don't eat **meat** or fish.*

medicine *noun*
Medicine is something that you swallow to make you better when you are ill.
دوا
*The **medicine** saved his life.*

meet *verb*
meets, meeting, met
If you **meet** someone, you see them and you talk to them.
ملاقات کرنا
*I **met** my friends in town today.*

melon *noun*
melons
A **melon** is a large, soft, sweet fruit with a hard green or yellow skin.
خربوزہ
*We ate slices of **melon**.*

melt *verb*
melts, melting, melted
When something **melts**, it changes from a solid to a liquid as it becomes warmer.
پگھلنا
***Melt** the chocolate in a bowl.*

memory *noun*
memories
1 Your **memory** is the part of your mind that remembers things.
حافظہ
*He has a very good **memory** for numbers.*
2 A **memory** is something you remember about the past.
یادداشت
*They discussed their **memories** of their school days.*

men
➡ Look at **man**.
*He ordered his **men** to stop.*

mend *verb*
mends, mending, mended
If you **mend** something that is broken, you repair it.
سدھارنا، مرمت کرنا
*They **mended** the hole in the roof.*

mess *noun*
If something is a **mess**, it is not neat.
بےترتیب حالت
*After the party, the house was a **mess**.*

message *noun*
messages
A **message** is a piece of information that you send someone.
پیغام
*I got emails and **messages** from friends all over the world.*

messy *adjective*
messier, messiest
A person or thing that is **messy** is not neat.
بے ترتیب، خراب
*His writing is rather **messy**.*

met
➡ Look at **meet**.
*We **met** when we were on holiday.*

A B C D E F G H I J K L M N O P Q R S T U V W X Y Z

metal *noun*
metals
Metal is a hard material that melts when it gets very hot.
دھات
*Gold, iron and lead are different kinds of **metal**.*

metre *noun*
metres
A **metre** is used for measuring distances or how long things are.
میٹر
*The hole in the ground is about one and a half **metres** across.*

mice
⇨ Look at **mouse**.
*You can hear the **mice** under the floor.*

midday *noun*
Midday is twelve o'clock in the middle of the day.
نصف النہار
*At **midday** everyone had lunch.*

middle *noun*
middles
The **middle** of something is the part that is the same distance from each edge or end.
درمیان
*We stood in the **middle** of the room.*

midnight *noun*
Midnight is twelve o'clock at night.
نصف شب
*They went to bed after **midnight**.*

might *verb*
You use **might** when something is possible.
سکنا
*He **might** win the race.*

mile *noun*
miles
A **mile** is used for measuring distance.
میل
*They drove 600 **miles** across the desert.*

milk *noun*
Milk is the white liquid that all baby mammals get from their mothers. People also drink **milk** that farmers get from cows.
دودھ
*They make cheese from goat's and sheep's **milk** too.*

millilitre *noun*
millilitres
A **millilitre** is used for measuring liquid. There are 1,000 **millilitres** in a litre.
ملی لیٹر
*I gave him the medicine with a 5 **millilitre** spoon.*

millimetre *noun*
millimetres
A **millimetre** is used for measuring how long things are. There are 1,000 **millimetres** in a metre.
ملی میٹر (میٹر کا ہزارواں حصہ)
*The small insect was a few **millimetres** long.*

mind *noun*
minds
Your **mind** is the part of your brain that thinks, understands and remembers.
دماغ
*I can't get that song out of my **mind**.*

mind *verb*
minds, minding, minded
If you **mind** something, it annoys you.
خیال کرنا
*It was hard work but she didn't **mind**.*

mine
Mine means belonging to me.
میرا
*That isn't your bag, it's **mine**.*

mine *noun*
mines
A **mine** is a deep hole or tunnel where people go to dig things like gold or diamonds out of rock.
کان، کھان

minus
You use **minus** when you take one number away from another number.
گھٹانا
*Three **minus** two is one.*

minute *noun*
minutes
A **minute** is used for measuring time. There are sixty seconds in one **minute**.
منٹ
*The food will take 20 **minutes** to cook.*

minute *adjective*
Something that is **minute** is very small.
معمولی، تھوڑی سی
*You only need to use a **minute** amount of glue.*

miss *verb*
misses, missing, missed
1 If you **miss** something that you are trying to hit or catch, you do not manage to hit it or catch it.
چھوٹ جانا
*I jumped, but **missed** the ball.*
2 If you **miss** something, you do not notice it.
دھیان نہ دینا، چوک جانا
*What did he say? I **missed** it.*
3 If you **miss** someone who is not with you, you feel sad that they are not there.
کمی محسوس کرنا
*The boys **miss** their father.*

Miss
You use **Miss** in front of the name of a girl or a woman who is not married when you are talking to her or talking about her.
آنسہ، مس
*Do you know **Miss** Smith?*

mistake *noun*
mistakes
A **mistake** is something that is not correct.
غلطی
*I made three **mistakes** in my letter.*

mix *verb*
mixes, mixing, mixed
If you **mix** things, you put different things together to make something new.
ملانا، خلط ملط کرنا
***Mix** the sugar with the butter.*

mixture *noun*
mixtures
A **mixture** is what you make when you mix different things together.
مرکب
*The drink is a **mixture** of orange and apple juice.*

mobile phone *noun*
mobile phones
A **mobile phone** is a small phone that you can take everywhere with you.
موبائل فون

model *noun*
models
1 A **model** is a small copy of something.
نمونہ
*I made the **model** house with paper and glue.*
2 A **model** is a person whose job is to wear and show new clothes.
ماڈل، شخصی نمونہ
*The **model** in the picture was very tall.*

mole *noun*
moles
1 A **mole** is a natural dark spot on your skin.
تل
*She has a **mole** on the side of her nose.*
2 A **mole** is a small animal with black fur that lives under the ground.
چھچھوندر

A B C D E F G H I J K L M N O P Q R S T U V W X Y Z

moment *noun*
moments
A **moment** is a very short period of time.
پل، لمحہ
*He stopped for a **moment**.*

Monday *noun*
Mondays
Monday is the day after Sunday and before Tuesday.
پیر
*I went back to school on **Monday**.*

money *noun*
Money is what you use to buy things.
رقم
*Cars cost a lot of **money**.*

monkey *noun*
monkeys
A **monkey** is an animal that has a long tail and can climb trees.
بندر

monster *noun*
monsters
In stories, a **monster** is a big, ugly creature that frightens people.
عفریت
*The film is about a **monster** in the wardrobe.*

month *noun*
months
A **month** is one part of a year. There are twelve **months** in one year.
ماہ
*We are going on holiday next **month**.*

moon *noun*
moons
The **moon** shines in the sky at night and moves around the earth every month.
چاند
*The first man on the **moon** was Neil Armstrong.*

more
You use **more** to talk about a greater amount of something.
مزید، زیادہ
*He has **more** chips than me.*

morning *noun*
mornings
The **morning** is the early part of the day, before lunch.
صبح
*What do you want to do tomorrow **morning**?*

most
1 **Most** of a group of things or people means nearly all of them.
زیادہ تر
***Most** of the houses here are very old.*
2 The **most** means the largest amount.
زیادہ
*Who has the **most** money?*

moth *noun*
moths
A **moth** is an insect like a butterfly that usually flies at night.
پروانہ، پتنگا

mother *noun*
mothers
A **mother** is a woman who has a child.
ماں

motorbike *noun*
motorbikes
A **motorbike** is a large bike with an engine.
موٹربائیک، موٹر سائیکل

motorway *noun*
motorways

A **motorway** is a wide road for travelling long distances fast.

چوڑی سڑک

mountain *noun*
mountains

A **mountain** is a very high area of land with steep sides.

پہاڑ، کوہ

*Ben Nevis is the highest **mountain** in Scotland.*

mouse *noun*
mice

1. A **mouse** is a small animal with a long tail.
   چوہا
2. You use a **mouse** to move things on a computer screen.
   ماؤس (کمپیوٹر کا)

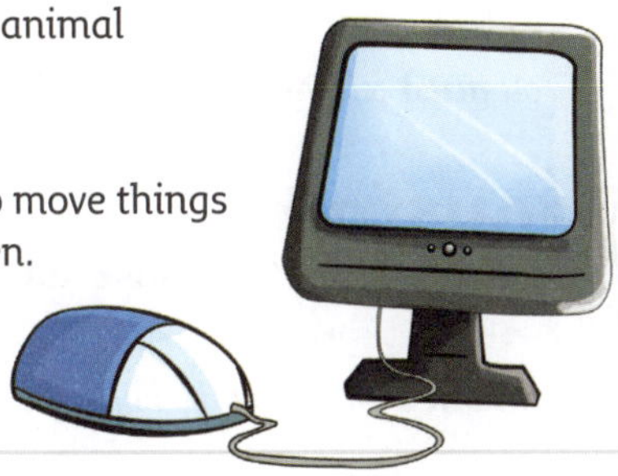

mouth *noun*
mouths

Your **mouth** is the part of your face that you use for eating or talking.

منہ

*When you cough, please cover your **mouth**.*

move *verb*
moves, moving, moved

1. When you **move** something, you put it in a different place.
   منتقل کرنا، حرکت دینا
   *The man asked her to **move** her car.*
2. If you **move**, you go to live in a different place.
   منتقل ہونا، گھر بدلنا
   *She's **moving** to London next month.*

Mr

You use **Mr** before a man's name when you are talking to him or talking about him.

مسٹر

*Our history teacher's name is **Mr** Jones.*

Mrs

You use **Mrs** before a married woman's name when you are talking to her or talking about her.

مسز

*How are you, **Mrs** Smith?*

Ms

You use **Ms** before a woman's name when you are talking to her or talking about her.

مِز

*The message is for **Ms** Clark.*

much

You use **much** to talk about a large amount of something.

زیادہ

*I ate too **much** food.*

mud *noun*

Mud is a mixture of earth and water.

کیچڑ

*There was thick **mud** on my football boots.*

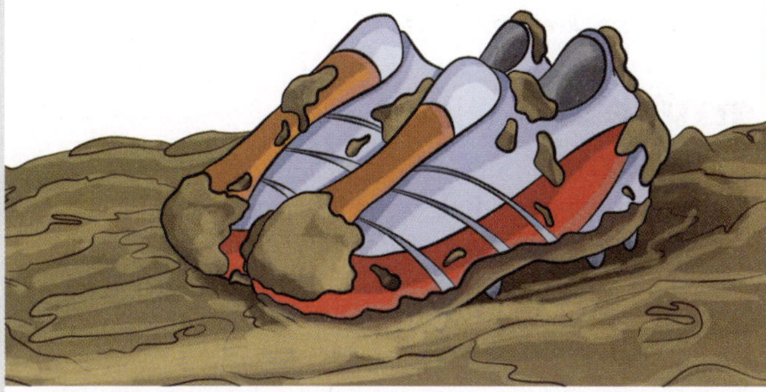

muddy *adjective*
muddier, muddiest

If something is **muddy**, it is covered with mud.

کیچڑ سے سنا ہوا

*My boots are all **muddy**!*

mug *noun*
mugs

A **mug** is a deep cup with straight sides.

مگ، پیالی

*He poured tea into the **mugs**.*

multiplication *noun*

Multiplication is when you multiply one number by another.

ضرب

multiply *verb*

multiplies, multiplying, multiplied

If you **multiply** a number, you add it to itself a number of times.

ضرب دینا

*You get 24 if you **multiply** three by eight.*

mum or mummy *noun*

mums or **mummies**

Mum or **mummy** is a name for your mother.

ماں

muscle *noun*

muscles

Your **muscles** are the parts inside your body that help you move.

پٹھا، عضلہ

*Sport helps to keep your **muscles** strong.*

museum *noun*

museums

A **museum** is a building where you can look at interesting, old, and valuable things.

عجائب گھر

*Hundreds of people came to the **museum** to see the dinosaur bones.*

mushroom *noun*

mushrooms

A **mushroom** is a plant with a short stem and a round top that you can eat.

ککر متا

*There are many types of wild **mushroom**, and some of them are poisonous.*

music *noun*

Music is the sound that you make when you sing or play instruments.

موسیقی

*What's your favourite **music**?*

musical instrument *noun*

musical instruments

A **musical instrument** is an instrument that you use to play music, like a piano or a guitar.

ساز، آلات موسیقی

must *verb*

You use **must** to show that you think something is very important.

ضروری ہونا

*You **must** tell the police all the facts.*

mustn't

Mustn't is short for **must not**.

نہیں چاہیے (لازم)

*I **mustn't** forget to take my key with me.*

my

You use **my** to show that something belongs to you.

میرا

*I went to sleep in **my** room.*

myself

You use **myself** when the you are talking about yourself.

میں خود

*I hurt **myself** when I fell down.*

mystery *noun*

mysteries

A **mystery** is something that you do not understand or know about.

اسرار، راز

*Why she's crying is a **mystery**.*

myth *noun*

myths

A **myth** is a very old story about magic, and strange people and creatures.

اساطیری کہانی، خیالی قصہ، داستان، دیومالا

Nn

nail *noun*
nails

1. A **nail** is a thin piece of metal. It is flat at one end and it has a point at the other end.
   کیل، میخ
   *A picture hung on a **nail** in the wall.*
2. Your **nails** are the thin hard parts that grow at the ends of your fingers and toes.
   ناخن
   *Try to keep your **nails** short.*

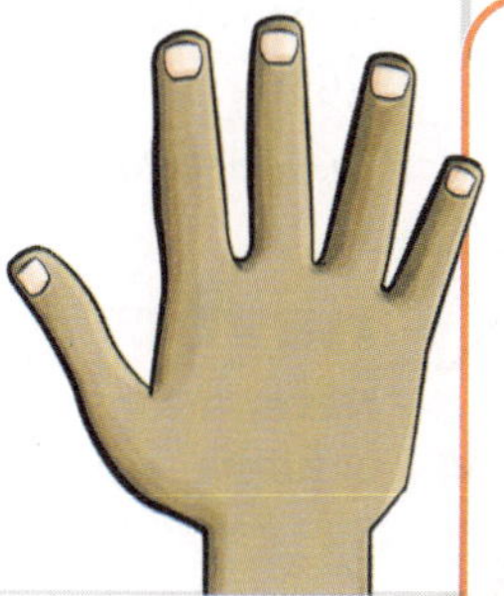

name *noun*
names

A person's **name** is the word or words that you use to talk to them, or to talk about them.
نام
*Is your **name** Peter?*

narrow *adjective*
narrower, narrowest

Something that is **narrow** is a small distance from one side to the other.
تنگ
*We walked through the town's **narrow** streets.*

nasty *adjective*
nastier, nastiest

Something that is **nasty** is horrible.
ناگوار
*That's a **nasty** thing to say!*

natural *adjective*

Natural things come from nature.
فطری، قدرتی
*The **natural** home of these animals is under the ground.*

nature *noun*

Nature is all the animals, plants, and other things in the world that people did not make or change.
فطرت، قدرت
*We watched **nature** all around us from our camp in the forest.*

naughty *adjective*
naughtier, naughtiest

A **naughty** child does things which are bad.
شوخ، شرارتی
*She was so **naughty**, her mother sent her to bed early.*

near *adjective*
nearer, nearest

If something is **near** a place, thing, or person, it is not far away from them.
قریب
*We are very **near** my house.*

nearly

Nearly means almost.
تقریباً
*It's **nearly** five o'clock.*

neat *adjective*
neater, neatest

A **neat** place or person is clean and tidy.
صاف ستھرا
*She made sure that her room was **neat** before she left.*

neck *noun*
necks

Your **neck** is the part of your body between your head and the rest of your body.
گردن
*He wore a gold chain around his **neck**.*

A B C D E F G H I J K L M N O P Q R S T U V W X Y Z

necklace *noun*
necklaces
A **necklace** is a chain of beads or jewels that you wear around your neck.
گلے کا ہار
*She's wearing a beautiful **necklace**.*

need *verb*
needs, needing, needed
If you **need** something, you believe that you must have it or do it.
ضرورت ہونا
*I **need** some more money.*

needle *noun*
needles
A **needle** is a small, thin metal tool with a sharp point that you use for sewing.
سوئی
*If you get me a **needle** and thread, I'll sew the button on.*

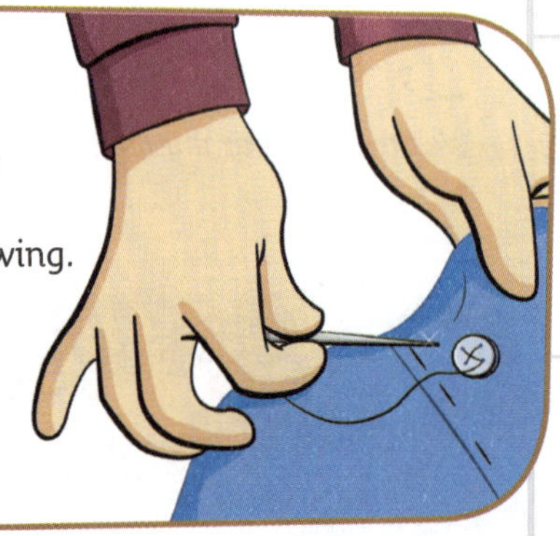

needn't
Needn't is short for **need not**.
ضرورت نہیں ہونا
*You **needn't** come with us if you don't want to.*

neighbour *noun*
neighbours
Your **neighbours** are the people who live around you.
پڑوسی
*I met our **neighbour** when I went to the shops.*

nephew *noun*
nephews
Someone's **nephew** is the son of their sister or brother.
بھتیجہ، بھانجہ
*I have a **nephew** who is still a baby.*

nervous *adjective*
If you are **nervous** about something, it worries you and you are rather afraid.
حوصلہ شکستہ
*I tried not to show that I was **nervous**.*

nest *noun*
nests
A **nest** is the place where a bird keeps its eggs or its babies.
گھونسلہ
*There were six small eggs in the bird's **nest**.*

net *noun*
nets
A **net** is made from pieces of string or rope tied together with holes between them. It is for catching things like fish, or the ball in some sports.
مچھر دانی
*The idea is to throw the ball into the top of the **net**.*

never
Never means at no time in the past, present or future.
کبھی نہیں
***Never** look straight at the sun.*

new *adjective*
newer, newest

1. Something that is **new** was not there before.
   نیا / نئی
   *They discovered a **new** medicine for his illness.*
2. If something is **new**, nobody has used it before.
   نیا
   *I am wearing my **new** shoes.*
3. A **new** thing or person is a different one from the one you had before.
   نیا / نئی
   *We have a **new** history teacher.*

news *noun*
News is information that you did not know before.
خبر
*We waited and waited for **news** of him.*

newspaper *noun*
newspapers
A **newspaper** is a number of large sheets of paper with news and other information printed on them.
اخبار
*They read about it in the **newspaper**.*

next *adjective*
The **next** thing is the one that comes immediately after this one or after the last one.
اگلا، اگلے
*I got up early the **next** morning.*

nice *adjective*
nicer, nicest
If something is **nice**, you like it.
نفیس
*They live in a really **nice** house.*

niece *noun*
nieces
Someone's **niece** is the daughter of their sister or brother.
بھتیجی، بھانجی
*He bought a present for his **niece**.*

night *noun*
nights
The **night** is the time when it is dark outside, and most people sleep.
رات
*It's eleven o'clock at **night** in Beijing.*

nightdress *noun*
nightdresses
A **nightdress** is a loose dress that a woman or girl can wear to sleep in.
لباسِ شب خوابی

nightmare *noun*
nightmares
A **nightmare** is a dream that frightens or worries you.
ڈراونا خواب یا تجربہ
*She had a **nightmare** last night.*

nine
Nine is the number **9**.
نو

no
You use **no** to say that something is not true or to refuse something.
نہیں
*"Would you like a drink?"—"**No** thank you."*

nobody *noun*
Nobody means not one person.
کوئی نہیں
*For a long time, **nobody** spoke.*

nod *verb*
nods, nodding, nodded
When you **nod**, you move your head up and down, usually to show that you agree.
سر ہلا کر رضامندی دینا
*She **nodded** and smiled.*

noise *noun*
noises
A **noise** is a loud sound.
شور
*Suddenly there was a **noise** like thunder.*

noisy *adjective*
noisier, noisiest
A **noisy** person or thing makes a lot of loud noise.
شور کرنے والا
*It was a very **noisy** party.*

none
None means not one or not any.
کوئی نہیں
***None** of us knew her.*

nonsense *noun*
If something is **nonsense**, it is not true or it is silly.
بکواس، بے معنی
*My father said the story was **nonsense**.*

noon *noun*
Noon is twelve o'clock in the middle of the day.
دوپہر
*The lesson started at **noon**.*

north *noun*
The **north** is the direction to your left when you are looking towards the place where the sun rises.
شمال

nose *noun*
noses
Your **nose** is the part of your face above your mouth that you use for breathing and for noticing smells.
ناک
*She sneezed and blew her **nose**.*

nostril *noun*
nostrils
Your **nostrils** are the two holes at the end of your nose.
نتھنا
*Keeping your mouth closed, breathe in through your **nostrils**.*

note *noun*
notes
1 A **note** is a short letter or message.
نوٹ، یادداشت کیلئے مختصر نکات لکھنا
*He wrote her a **note** and left it on the table.*
2 A **note** is one musical sound.
سر (موسیقی کا)
*She played some **notes** on her recorder.*

nothing
Nothing means not anything.
کچھ بھی نہیں
*There was **nothing** to do.*

notice *verb*
notices, noticing, noticed
If you **notice** something, you suddenly see or hear it.
معلوم ہونا، پتہ لگنا
*Did you **notice** him leave the room?*

notice *noun*
notices
A **notice** is a sign that gives information or instructions.
اطلاع
*The **notice** said "Please close the door."*

noun *noun*
nouns
A **noun** is a word that is used for talking about a person or thing. Examples of **nouns** are "child", "table", "sun", and "strength".
اِسم

November *noun*
November is the month after October and before December. It has 30 days.
نومبر

now
You use **now** to talk about the present time.
اب
*I must go **now**.*

nowhere
Nowhere means not anywhere.
کہیں بھی نہیں
*There's **nowhere** quiet for me to do my homework.*

number *noun*
numbers
A **number** is a word that you use to count.
عدد
*What **number** is your house?*

nurse *noun*
nurses
A **nurse** is a person whose job is to care for people who are ill.
نرس
*She thanked the **nurses** at the hospital.*

nut *noun*
nuts
A **nut** is a dry fruit with a hard shell.
اخروٹ
***Nuts** and seeds are very good for you.*

A B C D E F G H I J K L M N O P Q R S T U V W X Y Z

Oo

oak *noun*
oaks
An **oak** tree is a big, tall tree with a wide trunk. Its wood is good for making furniture.

oar *noun*
oars
An **oar** is a long piece of wood with a wide, flat end, used for moving a boat through the water.
چپو

obey *verb*
obeys, obeying, obeyed
If you **obey** a person or an order, you do what you are told to do.
فرماں برداری کرنا

ocean *noun*
oceans
An **ocean** is a big sea.
سمندر
*We crossed the Atlantic **Ocean**.*

o'clock *noun*
You say **o'clock** when saying what time it is.
بجے
*It is eight **o'clock** in the morning.*

octagon *noun*
octagons
An **octagon** is a shape with eight straight sides.
ہشت پہلو

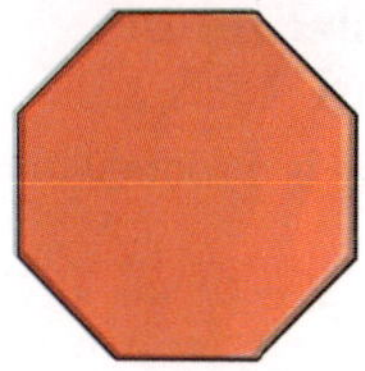

October *noun*
October is the month after September and before November. It has 31 days.
اکتوبر

octopus *noun*
octopuses
An **octopus** is a soft ocean animal with eight long arms.
اوکٹوپس (آٹھ ہاتھ والا آبی جندار)

odd *adjective*
odder, oddest
1 If something is **odd**, it is strange or unusual.
اجنبی، غیر معمولی، مناسب نہ ہونا، بے جوڑ
*There was an **odd** smell in the kitchen.*
2 You say that two things are **odd** when they do not belong to the same set or pair.
بے جوڑ، الگ
*I'm wearing **odd** socks.*
3 **Odd** numbers, such as 3 and 17, are numbers that cannot be divided by the number two.
طاق (عدد)

off
1 If you take something **off** another thing, it is no longer on it.
ہٹانا
*He took his feet **off** the desk.*
2 When something that uses electricity is **off**, it is not using electricity.
بند
*The light was **off**.*

offer *verb*
offers, offering, offered
If you **offer** something to someone, you ask them if they would like to have it.
پیشکش
*He **offered** his seat to the young woman.*

office *noun*
offices

An **office** is a room where people work at desks.

دفتر

often

Something that happens **often** happens many times or a lot of the time.

اکثر

oil *noun*

Oil is a thick liquid.

تیل

*We need some cooking **oil**.*

old *adjective*
older, oldest

1 An **old** person is someone who has lived for a long time.

بوڑھا / بوڑھی، عمر رسیدہ

*An **old** lady sat next to me.*

2 An **old** thing is something that somebody made a long time ago.

پرانا / پرانی

*We have a very **old** car.*

on

1 If someone or something is **on** a surface, it is resting there.

پر (ہونا)

*There was a large box **on** the table.*

2 When something that uses electricity is **on**, it is using electricity.

چالو، چلتی حالت میں

*The television is **on**.*

once

If something happens **once**, it happens one time only.

ایک بار

*I met her **once**, at a party.*

one *noun*

One is the number 1.

ایک

onion *noun*
onions

An **onion** is a small, round vegetable with a brown skin like paper and a very strong taste.

پیاز

only

1 If you talk about the **only** thing or person, you mean that there are no others.

صرف، واحد

*It was the **only** shop in the town.*

2 You use **only** when you are saying how small or short something is.

صرف

*Their house is **only** a few miles from here.*

3 If you are an **only** child, you have no brothers or sisters.

اکیلا / اکیلی

open *verb*
opens, opening, opened

1 When you **open** something, or when it **opens**, you move it so that it is no longer closed.

کھلا

*She **opened** the door.*

2 When a shop or office **opens**, people are able to go in.

کھلنا

*The banks will **open** again on Monday morning.*

opposite

1 If one thing is **opposite** another, it is across from it.

سامنے، بالمقابل

*Jennie sat **opposite** Sam at breakfast.*

2 If things are **opposite**, they are as different as they can be.

الٹا، معکوس، پیچھے کی طرف

*We watched the cars driving in the **opposite** direction.*

orange *noun*

1 An **orange** is a round fruit with a thick skin and lots of juice.

نارنگی (پھل)

2 **Orange** is a colour between red and yellow.

نارنجی (رنگ)

*Tigers are **orange** with black stripes.*

orchestra *noun*
orchestras

An **orchestra** is a large group of people who play music together.

آرکیسٹرا (موسیقی گروپ)

*The **orchestra** began to play.*

order *verb*
orders, ordering, ordered

If you **order** someone to do something, you tell them to do it.

حکم دینا

*She **ordered** him to leave.*

ordinary *adjective*

Ordinary means not special or different in any way.

معمولی

*It was just an **ordinary** day.*

other *adjective*
others

Other people or things are different people or things.

دوسرا

*All the **other** children had gone home.*

our

You use **our** to show that something belongs to you and one or more other people.

ہمارا

***Our** house is near the school.*

ours

You use **ours** when you are talking about something that belongs to you and one or more other people.

ہماری، ہمارا

*That car is **ours**.*

out

1 If you go **out** of a place, you leave it.
باہر
*She ran **out** of the house.*

2 If you are **out**, you are not at home.
باہر
*I called you yesterday, but you were **out**.*

3 If a light is **out**, it is no longer shining.
غائب ہونا، چلا جانا
*All the lights were **out** in the house.*

outside

1 The **outside** of something is the part that covers the rest of it.
باہر کی طرف
*They are painting the **outside** of the building.*

2 If you are **outside**, you are not in a building.
باہر، گھر سے باہر
*Let's play **outside**.*

oval *adjective*

Oval things have a shape like an egg.

بیضوی

*She has an **oval** table.*

oven *noun*
ovens

An **oven** is the part of a cooker like a large metal box with a door.

اوون

over

1 If one thing is **over** another thing, the first thing is above or higher than the second thing.
پر (ہونا)
*There was a lamp **over** the table.*

2 If something is **over**, it has finished.
ختم ہونا
*The class is **over**.*

owe *verb*
owes, owing, owed

If you **owe** money to someone, you have to pay money to them.

قرضدار ہونا

*He **owes** him $50.*

owl *noun*
owls

An **owl** is a bird with large eyes that hunts at night.

الو

own

You use **own** to say that something belongs to you.

اپنا، ذاتی

*Jennifer wanted her **own** room.*

ox *noun*
oxen

An **ox** is a kind of bull that is used for carrying or pulling things.

بیل

A B C D E F G H I J K L M N O P Q R S T U V W X Y Z

Pp

pack *verb*
packs, packing, packed
When you **pack** a bag, you put clothes and other things into it, because you are going away.
پیک کرنا، اکٹھا کر کے تھیلے میں ڈالنا

paddle *noun*
paddles
A **paddle** is a short oar. You use it to move a small boat through water.
پیڈل

paddle *verb*
paddles, paddling, paddled
1 If someone **paddles** a boat, they move it using a paddle.
پیڈل چلانا
2 If you **paddle**, you walk in shallow water.
پانی پہ حرکت کرنا

page *noun*
pages
A **page** is one side of a piece of paper in a book, a magazine, or a newspaper.
صفحہ
*Turn to **page** 4.*

paid
⇨ Look at **pay**.
*Daddy **paid** for the sweets.*

pain *noun*
pains
Pain is the feeling that you have in a part of your body, because of illness or an accident.
درد
*I felt a sudden sharp **pain** in my ankle.*

painful *adjective*
If a part of your body is **painful**, it hurts.
درد بھرا
*His right knee is very **painful**.*

paint *noun*
paints
Paint is a liquid used to decorate buildings, or to make a picture.
رنگ
*Can I use some of your red **paint**?*

paint *verb*
paints, painting, painted
1 If you **paint** something on a piece of paper or cloth, you make a picture of it using paint.
رنگ سے تصویر بنانا
*He likes **painting** flowers.*
2 If you **paint** a wall or a door, you cover it with paint.
رنگ کرنا، رنگنا

painting *noun*
paintings
A **painting** is a picture made with paint.
رنگ اور برش سے بنائی گئی تصویر
*He's doing a **painting** of a bowl of fruit.*

pair *noun*
pairs
A **pair** of things is two things of the same size and shape that are used together.
جوڑا
*She wore a **pair** of plain black shoes.*

palace *noun*
palaces
A **palace** is a very large house where important people live.
محل

pale *adjective*
paler, palest
A **pale** colour is not strong or bright.
کمزور
*She's wearing a **pale** blue dress.*

palm *noun*
palms
1 A **palm** or a **palm tree** is a tree that grows in hot countries. It has long leaves at the top, and no branches.
تاڑ (پیڑ)
2 The **palm** of your hand is the inside part of your hand, between your fingers and your wrist.
ہتھیلی

panda *noun*
pandas
A **panda** is a large animal with black and white fur.
پانڈا (جانور)

pantomime *noun*
pantomimes
A **pantomime** is a play that has a funny story with music and songs.
موسیقی کھیل (بچوں کے لئے)

paper *noun*
papers

1 **Paper** is a material that you write on or wrap things with.
کاغذ
*He wrote his name down on a piece of **paper**.*
2 A **paper** is a newspaper.
اخبار

parcel *noun*
parcels
A **parcel** is something that is wrapped in paper.
پارسل

parent *noun*
parents
Your **parents** are your mother and father.
والدین

park *noun*
parks
A **park** is a place with grass and trees. People go to **parks** to take exercise or play games.
پارک، ٹہلنے یا ورزش کرنے اور کھیلنے کی جگہ

park *verb*
parks, parking, parked
When someone **parks** a car, they leave it somewhere.
گاڑی کھڑی کرنا
*They **parked** in the street outside the house.*

parrot *noun*
parrots
A **parrot** is a bird with a curved beak and bright feathers.
طوطا
***Parrots'** feet have two toes at the front and two at the back.*

part *noun*
parts
Part of something is a piece of it.
حصہ، جزو

party *noun*
parties
A **party** is a time when people meet to have fun.
پارٹی، جشن
*She's having a birthday **party**.*

pass *verb*
passes, passing, passed
1 When you **pass** someone, you go by them.
گزرنا
*We **passed** them on our way here.*
2 If you **pass** something to someone, you give it to them.
دینا، حوالے کرنا
*He **passed** a note to his friend.*
3 If you **pass** a test, you do well.
پاس کرنا، کامیاب ہونا

passenger *noun*
passengers
A **passenger** is a person who is travelling in a vehicle, but who is not driving.
سواری

past *noun*

The **past** is the period of time before now.

ماضی

*In the **past**, there weren't any computers.*

past

1 Something that is **past** a place is on the other side of it.

پیچھے

*It's just **past** the school there.*

2 You use **past** when you are telling the time.

باقی ہونا، بجا ہونا

*It was ten **past** eleven.*

pasta *noun*

Pasta is a mixture of flour, eggs, and water.

پاستہ

***Pasta** comes in lots of shapes, even letters of the alphabet.*

paste *verb*

pastes, pasting, pasted

1 If you **paste** something on to a surface, you stick it with glue.

چپکانا

2 If you **paste** words or pictures on a computer, you copy them from one place and put them somewhere new.

پیسٹ کرنا (کمپیوٹر)

*You can **paste** by holding down the Ctrl key and pressing V.*

pastry *noun*

Pastry is a mixture of flour, butter, and water. People make it flat and thin so that they can use it to make pies.

پیسٹری (کیک)

path *noun*

paths

A **path** is a strip of ground that people walk along.

راستہ (پاتھ)

*We followed the **path** along the cliff.*

patient *adjective*

If you are **patient**, you don't get angry quickly.

تحمل مزاج، برداشت کرنے والا، صابر

patient *noun*

patients

A **patient** is someone that a nurse or a doctor is looking after.

مریض

pattern *noun*

patterns

A **pattern** is a group of repeated shapes.

ترتیب

*The carpet had a **pattern** of light and dark stripes.*

paw *noun*

paws

The **paws** of an animal such as a cat, dog, or bear are its feet.

پنجہ

*The kitten was black with white **paws**.*

pay *verb*

pays, paying, paid

If you **pay** for something, you give someone an amount of money for it.

ادا کرنا

*Did you **pay** for those sweets?*

peach *noun*

peaches

A **peach** is a round fruit with a soft red and orange skin.

آڑو، شفتالو

peanut *noun*

peanuts

Peanuts are small nuts that you can eat.

مونگ پھلی

pear *noun*

pears

A **pear** is a fruit which is narrow at the top and wide and round at the bottom.

ناشپاتی

peas *noun*

Peas are small, round, green vegetables.

مٹر کے دانے

pebble *noun*
pebbles
A **pebble** is a small, smooth stone.
گوٹی

pedal *noun*
pedals
The **pedals** on a bicycle are the two parts that you push with your feet to make the bicycle move.
پیڈل (سائکل کا)

peel *noun*
The **peel** of a fruit is its skin.
چھلکا

peg *noun*
pegs
A **peg** is a small piece of metal or wood on a wall that you hang things on.
الگنی

pen *noun*
pens
A **pen** is a long thin tool that you use for writing with ink.
قلم

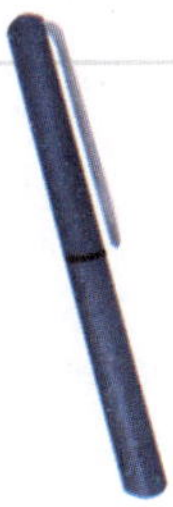

pencil *noun*
pencils
A **pencil** is a thin piece of wood with a black material through the middle that you use to write or draw with.
پینسل

penguin *noun*
penguins
A **penguin** is a black and white bird that lives in very cold places. **Penguins** can swim but they cannot fly.
پینگوئن

pentagon *noun*
pentagons
A **pentagon** is a shape with five straight sides.
پنج پہلو

people *noun*
People are men, women, and children.
لوگ
*Lots of **people** came to the party.*

pepper *noun*
peppers
1 **Pepper** is a powder with a hot taste that you put on food.
کالی مرچ
2 A **pepper** is a green, red, or yellow vegetable with seeds inside it.
مرچ، مرچی

period *noun*
periods
A **period** is a length of time.
وقفہ، مدت

person *noun*
people
A **person** is a man, a woman, or a child.
شخص

pest *noun*
pests
Pests are insects or small animals that damage crops or food.
کیڑا

pet *noun*
pets
A **pet** is a tame animal that you keep in your home.
پالتو

a b c d e f g h i j k l m n o p q r s t u v w x y z

A B C D E F G H I J K L M N O P Q R S T U V W X Y Z

petal *noun*
petals
The **petals** of a flower are the thin parts on the outside that are a bright colour.
پنکھڑی، پھول کی پتی

phone *noun*
phones
A **phone** is a piece of equipment that you use to talk to someone in another place.
فون
*Two minutes later the **phone** rang.*

photograph *noun*
photographs
A **photograph** is a picture that you take with a camera.
تصویر
*She took lots of **photographs** of her friends.*

piano *noun*
pianos
A **piano** is a large instrument for playing music. You play it by pressing the black and white keys.
پیانو (ساز)

pick *verb*
picks, picking, picked
1 If you **pick** someone, you choose them.
اٹھانا، لے جانا
2 When you **pick** flowers, fruit, or leaves, you take them from a plant or tree.
اتارنا، توڑنا
*I've **picked** some flowers from the garden.*

picnic *noun*
picnics
When people have a **picnic**, they eat a meal outside, usually in a park or a forest, or at the beach.
پکنک (تفریح)
*We're going on a **picnic** tomorrow.*

picture *noun*
pictures
A **picture** is a drawing or painting.
تصویر

pie *noun*
pies
A **pie** is a dish of fruit, meat, or vegetables that is covered with pastry and baked.
شامی کباب، ٹکیہ
*We each had a slice of apple **pie**.*

piece *noun*
pieces
A **piece** of something is a part of it.
ٹکڑا
*You must only take one **piece** of cake.*

pig *noun*
pigs
A **pig** is a farm animal with a fat body and short legs.
سور

pigeon *noun*
pigeons
A **pigeon** is a large grey bird.
کبوتر

pile *noun*
piles
A **pile** of things is several of them lying on top of each other.
ڈھیر
*We searched through the **pile** of boxes.*

pill *noun*
pills
Pills are small solid round pieces of medicine that you swallow.
گولی (دوا)

pillow *noun*
pillows
A **pillow** is something soft that you rest your head on when you are in bed.
تکیہ

pilot *noun*
pilots
A **pilot** is a person who controls an aircraft.
پائلٹ

pin *noun*
pins
A **pin** is a very small thin piece of metal with a point at one end.
پن

pineapple *noun*
pineapples
A **pineapple** is a large sweet yellow fruit with a lot of juice. Its skin is brown, thick, and very rough.
انناس

pipe *noun*
pipes
A **pipe** is a long tube that water or gas can flow through.
پائپ
*They are going to take out the old water **pipes**.*

pirate *noun*
pirates
Pirates are people who attack ships and steal things from them.
بحری قزاق
*They have to find the **pirates** and the hidden gold.*

pizza *noun*
pizzas
A **pizza** is a flat, round piece of bread. **Pizzas** are covered with cheese and tomatoes.
پزا
*Bake the **pizza** in a hot oven.*

place *noun*
places
1 A **place** is a building, area, town, or country.
جگہ، مقام
*This is the **place** where I was born.*
2 A **place** is also where something belongs.
جگہ، مقام
*He put the picture back in its **place** on the shelf.*

plain *adjective*
plainer, plainest
Something that is **plain** is ordinary and not special.
سادہ

plan *noun*
plans
A **plan** is a way of doing something that you work out before you do it.
منصوبہ
*I've got a **plan** for getting out of here.*

plane *noun*
planes
A **plane** is a large vehicle with wings and engines that flies through the air.
ہوائی جہاز، طیارہ

planet *noun*
planets
You find **planets** in space. They move around stars. The Earth is a **planet**.
کرہ، سیارہ

plant *noun*
plants
A **plant** is a living thing that grows in the earth. **Plants** have a stem, leaves, and roots.
پودا

plaster *noun*
plasters
1 A **plaster** is a strip of material with a soft part in the middle. You can cover a cut on your body with a **plaster**.
پلاسٹر، زخم پر لگانے والی پٹی
2 **Plaster** is a paste which people put on walls and ceilings so that they are smooth.
پلستر
*There were huge cracks in the **plaster**.*

plastic *noun*
Plastic is a material that is light but strong. It is made in factories.
پلاسٹک
*He put his sweets in a **plastic** bag.*

plate *noun*
plates
A **plate** is a flat dish that is used for holding food.
طشتری
*She pushed her **plate** away.*

platform *noun*
platforms
A **platform** in a station is the place where you wait for a train.
پلیٹ فارم

play *verb*
plays, playing, played
1 When you **play**, you spend time using toys and taking part in games.
کھیلنا
*She was **playing** with her dolls.*
2 If you **play** an instrument, you make music with it.
بجانا

playground *noun*
playgrounds
A **playground** is a special area where children can play.
کھیل کا میدان

please
You say **please** when you are asking someone to do something.
!برائے کرم
*Can you help us, **please**?*

plenty *noun*
If there is **plenty** of something, there is a lot of it.
ڈھیروں، بہت سا
*Don't worry. There's still **plenty** of time.*

plough *noun*
ploughs
A **plough** is a large tool that is used on a farm. Farmers pull it across a field to make the earth loose, so that they can plant seeds.
ہل (کھیت جوتنے کیلئے)

plus
You say **plus** to show that you are adding one number to another.
جمع
*Two **plus** two is four.*

pocket *noun*
pockets
A **pocket** is a small bag that is part of your clothes.
جیب
*He put the key in his **pocket**.*

poem *noun*
poems
A **poem** is a piece of writing. When people write a **poem**, they choose the words in a very careful way, so that they sound beautiful.
نظم

point *noun*
points
1 The **point** of something is its thin, sharp end. Needles and knives have **points**.
نوک
2 A **point** is a mark that you win in a game or a sport.
پوائنٹ

point *verb*
points, pointing, pointed
If you **point** at something, you stick out your finger to show where it is.
نشاندہی کرنا، اشارہ کرنا
*I **pointed** at the boy sitting near me.*

poisonous *adjective*
Something that is **poisonous** will kill you or hurt you if you swallow or touch it.
زہریلا

polar bear *noun*
polar bears
A **polar bear** is a large white bear which lives in the area around the North Pole.
قطبی بھالو

police
The **police** are the people who make sure that people obey the law.
پولس

polite *adjective*
Someone who is **polite** behaves well.
نرم خو

pond *noun*
ponds
A **pond** is a small area of water.
تالاب (انسان کا بنایا ہوا)
*We can feed the ducks on the **pond**.*

pony *noun*
ponies
A **pony** is a small horse.
گھوڑی (چھوٹے قد کی)

poor *adjective*
poorer, poorest
Someone who is **poor** doesn't have much money and doesn't own many things.
غریب

possible *adjective*
If something is **possible** it can happen.
ممکن

post *verb*
posts, posting, posted
If you **post** a letter, you put a stamp on it and send it to someone.
سپرد ڈاک کرنا، ڈاک سے بھیجنا

poster *noun*
posters
A **poster** is a large notice or picture that you stick on a wall.
پوسٹر

potato *noun*
potatoes
Potatoes are hard round white vegetables with brown or red skins. They grow under the ground.
آلو

pour *verb*
pours, pouring, poured
If you **pour** something like water, you make it flow out of a container.
انڈیلنا

powder *noun*
Powder is a fine dry dust, like flour.
سفوف

power *noun*
1 If someone has **power**, they have control over people.
اختیار
*He has the **power** to keep you in after school.*
2 The **power** of something is its strength.
قوت
*The engine doesn't often work at full **power**.*

practise *verb*
practises, practising, practised
If you **practise** something, you do it often in order to do it better.
عادی ہونا
*I've been **practising** my song.*

present *noun*
presents
1 The **present** is the period of time that is taking place now.
موجودہ وقت، حال میں
2 A **present** is something that you give to someone for them to keep.
موجود ہونا
*She got a **present** for her birthday.*

present *adjective*
If someone is **present** somewhere, they are there.
حاضر ہونا
*He wasn't **present** when they called out his name.*

press *verb*
presses, pressing, pressed
If you **press** something, you push it hard.
دبانا، دھکیلنا
***Press** the blue button.*

pretend *verb*
pretends, pretending, pretended
When you **pretend**, you act as if something is true, when you know it isn't.
تسلیم کروانا
*She **pretended** to be the teacher.*

pretty *adjective*
prettier, prettiest
If something is **pretty**, it is nice to look at.
پیارا، دلکش
*She was wearing a **pretty** necklace.*

price *noun*
prices
The **price** of something is how much you have to pay to buy it.
قیمتی
*Could you tell me the **price** of this car, please?*

prick *verb*
pricks, pricking, pricked
If you **prick** something, you stick something sharp like a pin or a knife into it.
چھوکر سوراخ کرنا
*She **pricked** her finger on a pin.*

prince *noun*
princes
A **prince** is a boy or a man in the family of a king or queen.
شہزادہ

princess *noun*
princesses
A **princess** is a girl or a woman in the family of a king or queen.
شہزادی

print *verb*
prints, printing, printed
1 If you **print** something, you use a machine to put words or pictures on paper.
پرنٹ کرنا، چھاپنا
2 If you **print** when you are writing, you do not join the letters together.
جلی حروف میں لکھنا

prison *noun*
prisons
A **prison** is a building where people who have broken the law are kept as a punishment.
جیل
*He was sent to **prison** for five years.*

prize *noun*
prizes
A **prize** is money or a special thing that you give to the person who wins a game, a race, or a competition.
اِنعام
*He won first **prize**.*

problem *noun*
problems
A **problem** is something or someone that makes thing difficult, or that makes you worry.
الجھن، دشواری

program *noun*
programs
A **program** is a set of instructions that a computer uses to do a job.
پروگرام (کمپیوٹر)

programme *noun*
programmes
A **programme** is a television or radio show.
پروگرام (ٹیلیویژن کا)
*She is watching her favourite television **programme**.*

project *noun*
projects
A **project** is a plan that takes a lot of time and effort.
منصوبہ بند کام
*It was a large building **project**.*

promise *verb*
promises, promising, promised
If you **promise** to do something, you say that you will be sure to do it.
وعدہ کرنا
*I **promise** that I'll help you all I can.*

pronoun *noun*
pronouns
A **pronoun** is a word that you use in place of a noun when you are talking about someone or something. "It" and "she" are **pronouns**.
ضمیر

proper *adjective*
The **proper** thing or way is the one that is right.
ٹھیک، حق
*Put things in their **proper** place.*

protect *verb*
protects, protecting, protected
If you **protect** something, you keep it safe.
حفاظت کرنا
*Make sure you **protect** your skin from the sun.*

proud *adjective*
prouder, proudest
If you feel **proud**, you feel pleased about something good that you or other people close to you have done.
فاخر
*I was **proud** of our team today.*

pudding *noun*
puddings
A **pudding** is something sweet that you eat after your main meal.
پڈنگ
*We had a delicious chocolate **pudding**.*

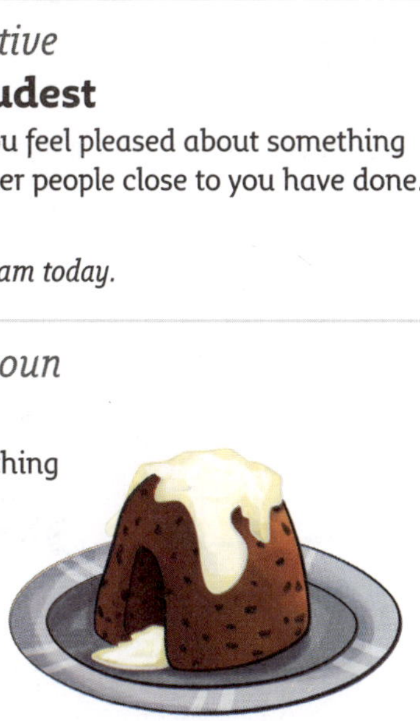

a b c d e f g h i j k l m n o p q r s t u v w x y z

A B C D E F G H I J K L M N O P Q R S T U V W X Y Z

puddle *noun*
puddles
A **puddle** is a small amount of water on the ground.
پانی بھرے گڑھے
Splashing in ***puddles*** *is lots of fun.*

pull *verb*
pulls, pulling, pulled
When you **pull** something, you hold it and move it towards you.
کھینچنا
The dentist had to ***pull*** *out all his teeth.*

punishment *noun*
punishments
Punishment is something done to someone because they have done something wrong.
سزا
His father sent him to bed early as a ***punishment*** *for being rude.*

pupil *noun*
pupils
The **pupils** at a school are the children who go there.
طالب علم
Around 200 ***pupils*** *go to this school.*

puppet *noun*
puppets
A **puppet** is a small model of a person or animal that you can move.
گڑیا

puppy *noun*
puppies
A **puppy** is a young dog.
پلہ

purple *noun*
Purple is a mixture of red and blue.
بینگنی
Some grapes are ***purple****.*

purse *noun*
purses
A **purse** is a small bag that women use to carry money and other things.
پرس (چرمی بیگ)
She reached in her ***purse*** *for her money.*

push *verb*
pushes, pushing, pushed
When you **push** something, you press it in order to move it away from you.
دھکہ دینا
I ***pushed*** *back my chair and stood up.*

put *verb*
puts, putting, put
When you **put** something somewhere, you move it there.
رکھنا
He ***put*** *the book on the desk.*

puzzle *verb*
puzzles, puzzling, puzzled
If something **puzzles** you, you do not understand it and you feel confused.
حیران کرنا
There was something about her that ***puzzled*** *me.*

pyjamas *noun*
Pyjamas are loose trousers and a jacket that you wear in bed.
لباسِ شب خوابی

pyramid *noun*
pyramids
A **pyramid** is a solid shape with a flat base and flat sides that make a point where they meet at the top.
ہرم، تکونی مقبرے

Qq

quack *verb*
quacks, quacking, quacked
When a duck **quacks**, it makes a loud sound.
بطخ کی آواز (قوئیک قوئیک)
*There were ducks **quacking** on the lawn.*

quarrel *noun*
quarrels
A **quarrel** is an angry argument between people.
جھگڑا
*I had an awful **quarrel** with my brothers.*

quarter *noun*
quarters
A **quarter** is one of four equal parts of something.
چوتھائی
*My sister ate a **quarter** of the chocolate cake.*

queen *noun*
queens
A **queen** is a woman who rules a country, or a woman who is married to a king.
ملکہ
*The crowd cheered when the **queen** went past.*

question *noun*
questions
A **question** is something that you say or write to ask a person about something.
سوال
*They asked her a lot of **questions** about her holiday.*

queue *noun*
queues
A **queue** is a line of people or cars waiting for something.
قطار
*He stood in the lunch **queue** for ten minutes.*

quick *adjective*
quicker, quickest
Something that is **quick** moves or does things with great speed.
تیز
*The cat was so **quick** that I couldn't catch it.*

quickly
If you move or do something **quickly** you do it with great speed.
تیزی سے
*The girl ran **quickly** along the street.*

quiet *adjective*
quieter, quietest
Someone who is **quiet** makes only a small amount of noise or no noise at all.
خاموش
*The baby was so **quiet** I didn't know he was there.*

quite
Quite means a bit but not a lot.
بالکل
*I **quite** like her but she's not my best friend.*

quiz *noun*
quizzes
A **quiz** is a game in which someone asks you questions to find out what you know.
مقابلہ سوال جواب
*After dinner we had a TV **quiz** and our team won.*

Rr

rabbit *noun*
rabbits

A **rabbit** is a small animal with long ears. **Rabbits** live in holes in the ground.

خرگوش

*The children were excited when they heard they were getting a pet **rabbit**.*

race *noun*
races

A **race** is a competition to see who is fastest, for example in running or driving.

دوڑ

*Nobody can beat my sister in a **race**.*

radiator *noun*
radiators

A **radiator** is a metal thing filled with hot water or steam. **Radiators** keep rooms warm.

ریڈیٹر (کار انجن کا حصہ)

*I burned myself on the **radiator** in the bathroom.*

radio *noun*
radios

A **radio** is a piece of equipment you use to hear programmes with talking, news and music.

ریڈیو

*Turn on the **radio** for the news please.*

railway *noun*
railways

A **railway** is a special road for trains, with stations along it. **Railways** have two metal lines that are always the same distance apart.

ریلوے

*The house was beside the **railway**.*

rain *noun*

Rain is water that falls from the clouds in small drops.

بارش

*My mother told me not to go out in the **rain**.*

rainbow *noun*
rainbows

A **rainbow** is a half circle of different colours in the sky. You can sometimes see a **rainbow** when it rains.

دھنک

*A **rainbow** appeared when the storm was over.*

ran

⇨ Look at **run**.

*I **ran** to school because I was late.*

rang

⇨ Look at **ring**.

*I got worried when the phone **rang**.*

rare *adjective*
rarer, rarest

Something that is **rare** is not seen or heard very often.

شاذونادر، شاذ وباذ

*We are lucky to see this bird because it is very **rare**.*

raspberry *noun*
raspberries

A **raspberry** is a small soft red fruit. **Raspberries** grow on bushes.

رس بھری

*Would you like some **raspberries** with your ice cream?*

rat *noun*
rats

A **rat** is an animal that looks like a mouse. A **rat** has a long tail and sharp teeth.

چوہا

*The old house was full of **rats**.*

rather

You use **rather** to mean "a little bit".

تھوڑا، تھوڑی

*I thought the party was **rather** boring.*

raw *adjective*

Raw food has not been cooked.

کچا

*There is a bowl of **raw** carrots and cauliflower on the table.*

reach *verb*

reaches, reaching, reached

1 When you **reach** a place, you arrive there.

رسائی پانا، پہنچنا

*We will not **reach** home until midnight.*

2 If you **reach** somewhere, you move your arm and hand to take or touch something.

پہنچنا

*I **reached** into my bag and brought out a pen.*

read *verb*

reads, reading, read

When you **read**, you look at written words and understand them, and sometimes say them aloud.

پڑھنا

*My father **reads** me a story every night before I go to sleep.*

ready *adjective*

If you are **ready**, you are able to do something or go somewhere right now.

آمادہ، تیار

*It takes her a long time to get **ready** for school.*

real *adjective*

1 Something that is **real** is true and is not imagined.

حقیقی

*No, it wasn't a dream. It was **real**.*

2 If something is **real**, it is not a copy.

اصلی

*Is your necklace **real** gold?*

really

1 You say **really** to show how much you mean something.

واقعی، درحقیقت

*I'm **really** sorry I can't come to your party.*

2 You say **really** to show that what you are saying is true.

واقعی، حقیقتاً

*Are we **really** going to the zoo?*

reason *noun*

reasons

The **reason** for something is the fact which explains why it happens.

وجہ

*You must have a good **reason** for being so late.*

receive *verb*

receives, receiving, received

When you **receive** something, someone gives it to you, or you get it after it has been sent to you.

حاصل کرنا

*Did you **receive** the birthday card I sent you?*

recipe *noun*

recipes

A **recipe** is a list of food and a set of instructions telling you how to cook something.

پکوان

*Do you have a **recipe** for chocolate cake?*

recite *verb*

recites, reciting, recited

When someone **recites** a poem or other piece of writing, they say it aloud after they have learned it.

بلند آواز میں خوش لحانی سے بولنا

*We each had to **recite** a poem in front of the class.*

record *noun*

records

A **record** is the best result ever.

ریکارڈ

*What's the world **record** for the 100 metres?*

record *verb*

records, recording, recorded

If you **record** something like a TV programme, you make a copy of it so that you can watch it later.

ریکارڈ کرنا، نقل کرنا، محفوظ کرنا

*Can you **record** the football for me please?*

recorder *noun*

recorders

A **recorder** is a small instrument in the shape of a pipe. You play a **recorder** by blowing into it and putting your fingers over the holes in it.

ریکارڈر

*He has been learning the **recorder** for three years.*

A B C D E F G H I J K L M N O P Q R S T U V W X Y Z

rectangle *noun*
rectangles
A **rectangle** is a shape with four straight sides.
مستطیل

red *noun*
Red is the colour of blood or a strawberry.
سرخ
Her dress is bright ***red****.*

reflection *noun*
reflections
A **reflection** is something you can see on a smooth, shiny surface. What you see is really in a different place.
انعکاس
Reflections *always show things the wrong way round.*

refuse *verb*
refuses, refusing, refused
If you **refuse** to do something, you say that you will not do it.
مسترد کرنا، انکار کرنا
He ***refuses*** *to have a bath.*

remember *verb*
remembers, remembering, remembered
If you **remember** people or things from the past, you can bring them into your mind and think about them.
یاد رکھنا، کرنا
I ***remember*** *the first time I met him.*

remind *verb*
reminds, reminding, reminded
If someone **reminds** you about something, they help you to remember it.
یاد دِلانا
Remind *me to buy a bottle of milk, will you?*

remove *verb*
removes, removing, removed
If you **remove** something from a place, you take it away.
ہٹانا، نکالنا
When the cake is cooked, ***remove*** *it from the oven.*

repair *verb*
repairs, repairing, repaired
If you **repair** something that is damaged or broken, you fix it so that it works again.
مرمت کرنا
The man managed to ***repair*** *the broken tap.*

repeat *verb*
repeats, repeating, repeated
If you **repeat** something, you say it, write it, or do it again.
دہرانا
Please can you ***repeat*** *the question?*

reply *verb*
replies, replying, replied
If you **reply** to something, you say or write an answer.
جواب دینا
Will you please ***reply*** *when I ask you a question.*

reptile *noun*
reptiles
A **reptile** is an animal that has cold blood, rough skin, and lays eggs. Snakes and lizards are **reptiles**.
حشرات

rescue *verb*
rescues, rescuing, rescued
If you **rescue** someone, you help them get away from a dangerous place.
راحت رسانی، مدد کرنا
The police ***rescued*** *20 people from the roof of the building.*

rest *verb*
rests, resting, rested
If you **rest**, you sit or lie down and do not do anything active for a while.
آرام کرنا
My grandmother always ***rests*** *in the afternoon.*

rest *noun*

The **rest** is the parts of something that are left.

باقی بچا ہوا

*Who ate the **rest** of the cake?*

restaurant *noun*

restaurants

A **restaurant** is a place where you can buy and eat a meal.

ریستوراں

*We had lunch in an Italian **restaurant**.*

result *noun*

results

A **result** is something that happens because another thing has happened.

نتیجہ

*I got measles and as a **result** was off school for two weeks.*

return *verb*

returns, returning, returned

1 When you **return** to a place, you go back to it after you have been away.

واپس ہونا

*He **returned** to Japan after his holiday in England.*

2 If you **return** something to someone, you give it back to them.

واپس کرنا

*I forgot to **return** my library books.*

reward *noun*

rewards

A **reward** is something that is given to a person because they have done something good.

صلہ

*The school gives **rewards** to children who behave well.*

rhinoceros *noun*

rhinoceroses

A **rhinoceros** is a large wild animal with thick grey skin. A **rhinoceros** has one or two horns on its nose.

گینڈا

rhyme *verb*

rhymes, rhyming, rhymed

If two words **rhyme**, they have the same sound at the end of them.

ہم قافیہ، ہم آواز

*Sally **rhymes** with valley.*

rhythm *noun*

rhythms

Rhythm is something which is repeated again and again in the same way.

لب ولہجہ

*Listen to the **rhythm** of the music.*

rib *noun*

ribs

Your **ribs** are the 12 pairs of curved bones that go round your body.

پسلی

*He fell off his bike and broke a **rib**.*

ribbon *noun*

ribbons

A **ribbon** is a long narrow piece of cloth. You use **ribbons** to decorate things or tie them together.

ربن

*The girl's hair was tied with a blue and white **ribbon**.*

rice *noun*

Rice is white or brown grains from a plant. **Rice** grows in wet areas.

چاول

*The meal was chicken, **rice**, and vegetables.*

rich *adjective*

richer, richest

Someone who is **rich** has a lot of money and expensive things.

امیر

*She is a **rich** woman who owns a very large house.*

riddle *noun*

riddles

A **riddle** is a question that seems to be nonsense, but that has a clever answer.

پہیلی

*He asked the **riddle**, "What key cannot open a door?" and I answered, "a monkey".*

A B C D E F G H I J K L M N O P Q R S T U V W X Y Z

ride *verb*

rides, riding, rode, ridden

When you **ride** a horse or a bike, you sit on it and control it as it moves along.

سواری کرنا

*The girl **rode** her horse along the beach.*

right *adjective*

1 If something is **right**, it is correct and there have been no mistakes.

درست، صحیح

*Only one child in the class knew the **right** answer to the teacher's question.*

2 The **right** side is the side that is towards the east when you look north.

دایاں، داہنا

*Most people write with their **right** hand.*

ring *verb*

rings, ringing, rang, rung

When a bell **rings**, it makes a clear, loud sound.

گھنٹی بجنا

*The school bell **rings** at nine o'clock.*

ring *noun*

rings

A **ring** is a round piece of metal that you wear on a finger.

گھنٹی

*He turned the **ring** on his finger.*

ripe *adjective*

riper, ripest

When fruit or grain is **ripe**, it is ready to be eaten.

پکا ہوا

*Don't eat the apples until they are **ripe**.*

rise *verb*

rises, rising, rose, risen

If something **rises**, it moves up.

اوپر اٹھنا

*We watched the balloon **rise** into the sky.*

river *noun*

rivers

A **river** is a long line of water that flows into the sea.

ندی

*The Nile is one of the longest **rivers** in the world.*

road *noun*

roads

A **road** is a long piece of hard ground for vehicles to travel on.

سڑک

*You must look both ways before you cross the **road**.*

roar *verb*

roars, roaring, roared

If a person, an animal or a thing **roars**, they make a very loud noise.

گرجنا

*The engines **roared** and the aeroplane started to move.*

robot *noun*

robots

A **robot** is a machine that can move and do things that it has been told to do.

روبوٹ

*We have **robots** that we could send to the moon.*

rock *noun*

rocks

1 **Rock** is the hard material that is in the ground and in mountains.

چٹان

*We tried to dig, but the ground was solid **rock**.*

2 A **rock** is a piece of this material.

کنکر، ڈھیلا

*She picked up a **rock** and threw it into the lake.*

rock *verb*

rocks, rocking, rocked

If something **rocks**, it moves from side to side.

شانہ بشانہ چلنا، ساتھ ساتھ چلنا، بغل میں چلنا

rocket *noun*

rockets

A **rocket** is a vehicle that people use to travel into space.

راکیٹ

*This is the **rocket** that took them to the moon.*

rode

⇨ Look at **ride**.

*The man **rode** his bike down the hill.*

roll *verb*
rolls, rolling, rolled

When something **rolls**, it moves along a surface, turning over and over.

لڑھکنا

*The ball bounced out of the garden and **rolled** across the road.*

roof *noun*
roofs

The **roof** of a building is the bit on top that covers it.

چھت

*Our house is the one with the red **roof**.*

room *noun*
rooms

1 A **room** is a part of a building that has its own walls.

کمرہ

*A minute later he left the **room**.*

2 If there is **room** somewhere, there is a enough empty space.

گنجائش، خالی جگہ

*There isn't **room** for any more furniture in here.*

root *noun*
roots

The **roots** of a plant are the parts of it that grow under the ground.

جڑ

*She dug a hole near the **roots** of an apple tree.*

rope *noun*
ropes

A **rope** is a type of very thick string that is made by twisting together several strings or wires.

رسی

*He tied the **rope** around his waist.*

rose *noun*
roses

A **rose** is a large garden flower with a lovely smell. **Roses** grow on bushes.

گلاب

*The teacher was given a bunch of red **roses**.*

rough *adjective*
rougher, roughest

1 If something is **rough**, it is not smooth or even.

کھردرا

*His hands were **rough**.*

2 If you are **rough**, you are not being careful or gentle.

غیر محتاط ہونا، سختی سے کرنا

*Don't be so **rough** or you'll break it.*

round *adjective*
rounder, roundest

Something **round** is in the shape of a ball or a circle.

گول، دائرہ نما

*There was a **round** table in the middle of the room.*

row *noun*
rows

A **row** is a line of things or people.

قطار

*Our house is opposite a **row** of shops.*

rub *verb*
rubs, rubbing, rubbed

If you **rub** something, you move your hand or a cloth backwards and forwards over it.

رگڑنا

*I **rubbed** the window and looked outside.*

rubber *noun*
rubbers

1 **Rubber** is a strong material that stretches. **Rubber** is used to make things like tyres and boots for wet weather.

ربر

2 A **rubber** is a small piece of rubber used to remove pencil mistakes.

ربر (پنسل کے نشانات مٹانے والا)

*Have you got a **rubber** in your pencil case?*

rubbish *noun*

Rubbish is things like empty packs and used paper that you throw away.

بکواس

rude *adjective*

ruder, rudest

If people are **rude**, they are not polite.

غیر مہذب

*It is **rude** to ask for something without saying "please".*

ruin *verb*

ruins, ruining, ruined

If you **ruin** something, you destroy or spoil it.

برباد کرنا، تباہ کرنا

*The rain **ruined** the party.*

rule *noun*

rules

Rules are instructions that tell you what you must do or must not do.

اصول، قواعد

*Can you explain the **rules** of cricket to me?*

rule *verb*

rules, ruling, ruled

Someone who **rules** a country controls it.

حکومت کرنا

ruler *noun*

rulers

1 A **ruler** is a long, flat piece of wood or plastic with straight edges. You use a **ruler** for measuring things or drawing straight lines.
پیمائش کا آلہ، رولر

2 A **ruler** is also a person who rules a country.
حکمراں
*He was **ruler** of France at that time.*

run *verb*

runs, running, ran, run

When you **run**, you move very quickly on your legs.

دوڑنا

*It's very dangerous to **run** across the road.*

rung

⇨ Look at **ring**.

*They had **rung** the door bell when I was in the shower.*

Ss

sad *adjective*

sadder, saddest

If you are **sad**, you don't feel happy.

ناخوش، اداس

*I'm **sad** that he is leaving.*

safe *adjective*

safer, safest

If you are **safe**, you are not in any danger.

محفوظ ہونا

*Is it **safe**?*

said

⇨ Look at **say**.

*That is what she **said** to me.*

sail *noun*

sails

Sails are large pieces of cloth on a boat that catch the wind and move the boat along.

بادبان

salad *noun*

salads

A **salad** is a mixture of vegetables and sometimes other foods. You usually eat **salads** cold.

سلاد

salt *noun*

Salt is a white powder that you use to make food taste better.

نمک

*Now add **salt** and pepper.*

same *adjective*

If two things are the **same**, they are like one another.

اس جیسا، یکساں

*The two cats look the **same**.*

sand *noun*

Sand is a powder made of very small pieces of stone. Deserts and most beaches are made of **sand**.

ریت

sandal *noun*

sandals

Sandals are light shoes that you wear in warm weather.

سینڈل (جوتے)

*He put on a pair of old **sandals**.*

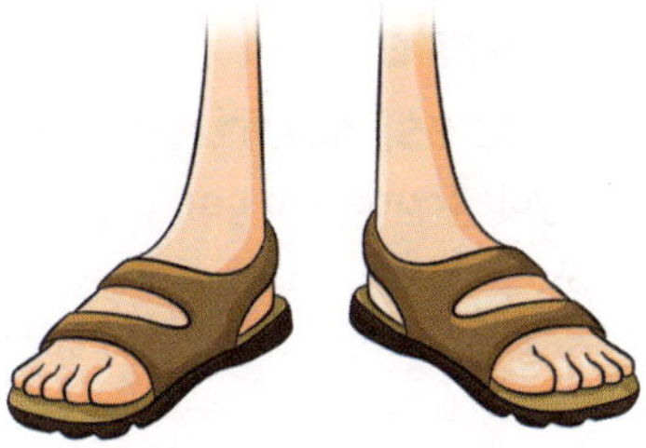

sandwich *noun*

sandwiches

A **sandwich** is two slices of bread with another food such as cheese or meat between them.

سینڈوچ (دوپرتی)

*She ate a large **sandwich**.*

sang

⇨ Look at **sing**.

*She **sang** a happy song.*

sank

⇨ Look at **sink**.

*The boat **sank** in the storm.*

sari *noun*

saris

A **sari** is a long piece of material worn folded around the body by women.

ساری

*She was wearing a new yellow **sari**.*

sat

⇨ Look at **sit**.

*She **sat** down next to the fire.*

satellite *noun*

satellites

A **satellite** is a machine that is sent into space to receive and send back information.

سیٹلائٹ، مصنوعی سیارہ

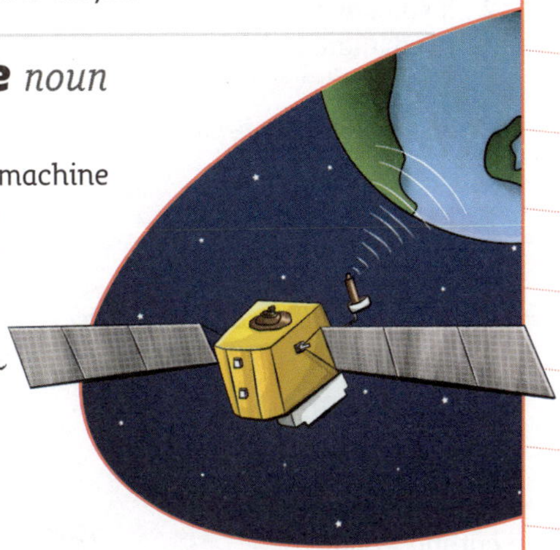

Saturday *noun*

Saturdays

Saturday is the day after Friday and before Sunday.

سنیچر

*He called her on **Saturday** morning.*

saucepan *noun*

saucepans

A **saucepan** is a deep metal container with a long handle and a lid. **Saucepans** are used for cooking.

ساس پین (دستہ والا برتن)

*Put the potatoes in a **saucepan** and boil them.*

saucer *noun*

saucers

A **saucer** is a small curved plate that you put under a cup.

طشتری

A B C D E F G H I J K L M N O P Q R S T U V W X Y Z

sausage *noun*

sausages

A **sausage** is a mixture of very small pieces of meat and other foods, inside a long thin skin.

سوسیج، قیمہ

save *verb*

saves, saving, saved

1 If you **save** someone or something, you help them to escape from danger.

بچانا

*He **saved** the boy from drowning.*

2 If you **save** something, you keep it because you will need it later.

محفوظ کرنا

*She was **saving** her money.*

saw

⇨ Look at **see**.

*We **saw** her walking down the street.*

saw *noun*

saws

A **saw** is a metal tool for cutting wood.

آری

*He used a **saw** to cut the branches off the tree.*

say *verb*

says, saying, said

When you **say** something, you talk.

کہنا

*She **said** that they were very pleased.*

scale *noun*

scales

Scales are small, flat pieces of hard skin that cover the body of animals like fish and snakes.

چھپرا (مچھلی یا سانپوں کے جسم پر پائی جانے والی کھال)

scales *noun*

Scales are a machine used for weighing things.

ترازو

*He weighed flour on the **scales**.*

scared *adjective*

If you are **scared** of something it frightens you.

خوفزدہ ہونا، ڈرنا

*She is **scared** of spiders.*

school *noun*

schools

A **school** is a place where people go to learn.

اِسکول

*The **school** was built in the 1960s.*

science *noun*

sciences

Science is the study of natural things.

سائنس

scissors *noun*

Scissors are a small tool for cutting with two sharp parts that are joined together.

قینچی

*Cut the card using **scissors**.*

score *verb*

scores, scoring, scored

If you **score** in a game, you get a goal, run, or point.

اسکور

*He **scored** his second goal of the game.*

scratch *verb*

scratches, scratching, scratched

1 If a sharp thing **scratches** someone or something, it makes small cuts on their skin or on its surface.

کھرچنا

*The branches **scratched** my face.*

2 If you **scratch** part of your body, you rub your nails against your skin.

کھجانا، کھجلی کرنا

*He **scratched** his head.*

scream *verb*

screams, screaming, screamed

If you **scream**, you shout or cry in a loud, high voice.

چلانا

*She **screamed** when she saw the spider.*

screen *noun*
screens
A **screen** is a flat surface on which a picture is shown.
اسکرین، پردہ
*There was dust on the television **screen**.*

sea *noun*
seas
A **sea** is a large area of salt water.
مجسمہ سازی، بت تراشی
*They swam in the warm **sea**.*

seal *verb*
seals, sealing, sealed
When you **seal** an envelope, you close it by folding part of it and sticking it down.
مہر بند کرنا، چپکا کر بند کر دینا
*He **sealed** the envelope and put on a stamp.*

search *verb*
searches, searching, searched
If you **search** for something or someone, you look for them everywhere.
تلاش
*I am **searching** for my glasses.*

seaside *noun*
The **seaside** is an area next to the sea.
سمندر کے قریب
*I went to spend a few days at the **seaside**.*

season *noun*
seasons
The **seasons** are the four parts of a year: spring, summer, autumn and winter.
موسم
*Spring is my favourite **season**.*

seat *noun*
seats
A **seat** is something that you can sit on.
سیٹ، نشست

second *adjective*
The **second** thing in a number of things is the one that you count as number two.
دوسرا
*It was the **second** day of his holiday.*

second *noun*
seconds
A **second** is an amount of time. There are sixty **seconds** in one minute.
سیکنڈ
*For a few **seconds** nobody spoke.*

secret *adjective*
If something is **secret**, only a small number of people know about it, and they do not tell any other people.
خفیہ، پوشیدہ
*He knew a **secret** place to hide in the garden.*

see *verb*
sees, seeing, saw, seen
1 If you **see** something, you are looking at it or you notice it.
دیکھنا
*The fog was so thick we couldn't **see** anything.*
2 If you **see** someone, you meet them.
ملاقات کرنا
*I **saw** him yesterday.*

seed *noun*
seeds
A **seed** is the small, hard part of a plant from which a new plant grows.
بیج
*Plant the **seeds** in the garden.*

seem *verb*
seems, seeming, seemed
If something **seems** to be true, it appears to be true or you think it is true.
محسوس ہونا
*The thunder **seemed** very close.*

seen

⇨ Look at **see**.

*She had **seen** the film before.*

sell *verb*

sells, selling, sold

If you **sell** something, you let someone have it in return for money.

فروخت کرنا

*The man **sold** his bike.*

semicircle *noun*

semicircles

A **semicircle** is a half of a circle, or something with this shape.

دائرے کا نصف

*The children stood in a **semicircle**.*

send *verb*

sends, sending, sent

When you **send** someone a message or a parcel, you make it go to them.

بھیجنا

*I will **send** you a letter when I arrive.*

sensible *adjective*

If you do something **sensible**, you have thought about it a lot first.

حساس

*The **sensible** thing is not to touch it.*

sent

⇨ Look at **send**.

*He **sent** a letter home.*

September *noun*

September is the month after August and before October. It has 30 days.

ستمبر

serve *verb*

serves, serving, served

Someone who **serves** customers in a shop or a restaurant helps them with what they want to buy.

پیش کرنا

*She **served** me coffee and pie.*

set *noun*

sets

A **set** of things is a number of things that belong together.

سیٹ (ایک گروپ کی چیزیں)

*I'll need a **set** of clean clothes.*

seven

Seven is the number 7.

سات

several *adjective*

You use **several** for talking about a number of people or things that is not large but is greater than two.

متعدد، کئی

*There were **several** boxes on the table.*

sew *verb*

sews, sewing, sewed, sewn

When you **sew** pieces of cloth together, you join them using a needle and thread.

سینا، سلائی کرنا

*I must **sew** a button on to this shirt.*

sex *noun*

sexes

The **sex** of a person or animal is if it is male or female.

جنس

*What **sex** is the baby?*

shadow *noun*
shadows

A **shadow** is a dark shape on a surface that is made when something blocks the light.

پرچھائی

*The **shadows** of the trees crossed their path.*

shake *verb*
shakes, shaking, shook, shaken

1. If you **shake** something, you hold it and move it quickly up and down.

   ہلانا

   ***Shake** the bottle before you drink.*
2. If someone or something **shakes**, they move quickly backwards and forwards or up and down.

   کانپنا، تھرتھرانا

   *My body was **shaking** with cold.*

shallow *adjective*
shallower, shallowest

If something is **shallow**, it is not deep.

کم گہرا

*The river is very **shallow** here.*

shape *noun*
shapes

The **shape** of something is the way its outside edges or surfaces look.

شکل

*Pasta comes in different **shapes** and sizes.*

share *verb*
shares, sharing, shared

If you **share** something with another person, you both have it or use it.

اشتراک کرنا، مل جل کر استعمال کرنا

*We **shared** an ice cream.*

shark *noun*
sharks

A **shark** is a very large fish. **Sharks** have very sharp teeth and some may attack people.

شارک (بڑی مچھلی)

sharp *adjective*
sharper, sharpest

1. A **sharp** point or edge is very thin and can cut through things quickly.

   تیزدھار

   *Be careful, the scissors are **sharp**.*
2. A **sharp** feeling is sudden and is very big or strong.

   تیز

   *I felt a **sharp** pain in my right leg.*

shave *verb*
shaves, shaving, shaved

If you **shave**, you remove hair from your face or body by cutting it off.

چہرے کے بال صاف کرنا (شیو)

*Rahim took a bath and **shaved**.*

shed *noun*
sheds

A **shed** is a small building where you store things.

سائبان

*The house has a large **shed** in the garden.*

she'd

1. **She'd** is short for **she had**.

   اس نے (مونث ماضی)

   ***She'd** already seen them.*
2. **She'd** is also short for **she would**.

   اس نے (مونث ماضی شرطیہ)

   ***She'd** be very happy.*

sheep *noun*
sheep

A **sheep** is a farm animal with thick hair called wool. Farmers keep **sheep** for their wool or for their meat.

بھیڑ

sheet *noun*
sheets

1. A **sheet** is a large piece of cloth that you sleep on or cover yourself with in bed.

   چادر

   *Once a week, we change the **sheets**.*
2. A **sheet** is a piece of paper, glass, plastic, or metal.

   صفحات

   *He folded the **sheets** of paper.*

shelf *noun*

shelves

A **shelf** is a long flat piece of wood on a wall or in a cupboard that you can keep things on.

دراز، الماری

*Dad took a book from the **shelf**.*

shell *noun*

shells

1 The **shell** of an egg or nut is its hard part.

خول

2 The **shell** of an animal such as a snail is the hard part that covers its back and protects it.

خول (گھونگھے وغیرہ کا)

she'll

She'll is short for **she will**.

وہ (مؤنث مستقبل)

***She'll** be back.*

she's

She's is short for **she is**.

وہ (مؤنث حال)

***She's** a doctor.*

shine *verb*

shines, shining, shone

If something **shines**, it gives out bright light.

چمکنا

*Today it's warm and the sun is **shining**.*

shiny *adjective*

shinier, shiniest

If something is **shiny**, it is bright.

چمکدار

*Her hair was **shiny** and clean.*

ship *noun*

ships

A **ship** is a large boat that carries people or things.

جہاز (بحری)

*The **ship** was ready to leave.*

shirt *noun*

shirts

A **shirt** is something you wear on the top part of your body. It has a collar and buttons.

قمیض

shiver *verb*

shivers, shivering, shivered

If you **shiver**, your body shakes because you are cold or scared.

کانپنا

*She **shivered** with cold.*

shoe *noun*

shoes

Shoes are a type of clothing that you wear on your feet.

جوتا

*I need a new pair of **shoes**.*

shone

⇨ Look at **shine**.

*The sun **shone** all day.*

shop *noun*

shops

A **shop** is a place that sells things.

دکان

*He and his wife run a clothes **shop**.*

shore *noun*

shores

The **shore** of a sea or lake is the land along the edge of it.

کنارا

*They walked slowly down to the **shore**.*

short *adjective*

shorter, shortest

1 If something is **short**, it does not last very long.

مختصر

*Last year we all went to the seaside for a **short** holiday.*

2 A **short** thing is small in length, distance, or height.

چھوٹا قد

*She has **short**, straight hair.*

shorts *noun*

Shorts are trousers with short legs.

شورٹس، ہاف پینٹ

*He was wearing blue **shorts**.*

should *verb*

You use **should** when you are saying what is the right thing to do.

ہونا

*He **should** tell us what happened.*

shoulder *noun*

shoulders

Your **shoulders** are the two parts of your body between your neck and the tops of your arms.

کندھا

*Put your hands on the **shoulders** of the person in front of you.*

shout *verb*

shouts, shouting, shouted

If you **shout**, you say something in a very loud voice.

چلانا

*He **shouted** something to his brother.*

show *verb*

shows, showing, showed, shown

1 If you **show** someone something, you let them see it.

دکھانا

*She **showed** me her ring.*

2 If you **show** someone how to do something, you teach them how to do it.

کرکے دکھانا، کرکے بتانا، مظاہرہ کرنا

*She **showed** us how to make pasta.*

shower *noun*

showers

1 A **shower** is a thing that you stand under, that covers you with water so you can wash yourself.

شاور (غسل کیلئے)

*I was in the **shower** when the phone rang.*

2 A **shower** is a short period of rain.

پھوار پڑنا

*A few **showers** are expected tomorrow.*

shown

Look at **show**.

*I've **shown** them how to do it.*

shut *verb*

shuts, shutting, shut

If you **shut** something, you close it.

بند کرنا

*Please **shut** the gate.*

shy *adjective*

shyer, shyest

If you are **shy**, you are nervous about talking to people that you do not know well.

شرمیلی / شرمیلا

*She was a **shy**, quiet girl.*

sick *adjective*

sicker, sickest

If you are **sick**, you are not well.

بیمار

*He's very **sick** and needs a doctor.*

side *noun*

sides

1 The **side** of something is a place to the left or right of it.

پہلو، بغل

*On the left **side** of the door there's a door bell.*

2 The **side** of something is also its edge.

پہلو، بغل

*A square has four **sides**.*

3 The different **sides** in a game are the groups of people who are playing against each other.

پہلو

*Both **sides** want to win the match.*

a b c d e f g h i j k l m n o p q r s t u v w x y z

sign *noun*
signs

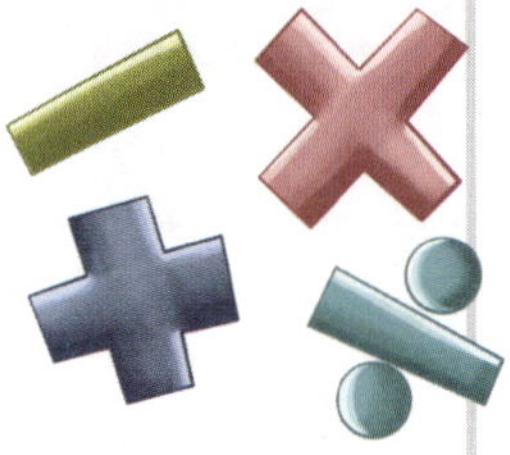

1 A **sign** is a mark or a shape that has a special meaning.
علامت، نشان
*In maths, + is a plus **sign** and - is a minus **sign**.*

2 You can also make a **sign** to somebody by moving something.
اشارہ کرنا
*They gave me a **sign** to show that everything was all right.*

silent *adjective*

1 If you are **silent**, you are not talking.
خاموش
*She was **silent** because she did not know what to say.*

2 If something is **silent**, it is quiet, with no sound at all.
خاموش، پرسکون
*The room was **silent**.*

silly *adjective*
sillier, silliest
If you are **silly**, you do not behave in a sensible way.
بیوقوف
*Don't be **silly**!*

silver *noun*
Silver is a valuable metal.
چاندی
*He bought her a bracelet made from **silver**.*

sing *verb*
sings, singing, sang, sung
When you **sing**, you make music with your voice.
گانا
*I love **singing**.*

sink *noun*
sinks
A **sink** is a large fixed container in a kitchen or a bathroom that you can fill with water.
سنک، برتن دھونے والی جگہ
*The **sink** was filled with dirty dishes.*

sister *noun*
sisters
Your **sister** is a girl or woman who has the same parents as you.
بہن
*This is my **sister**.*

sit *verb*
sits, sitting, sat
If you are **sitting** in a chair, your bottom is resting on the chair and the top part of your body is straight.
بیٹھنا
*Mum was **sitting** in her chair in the kitchen.*

six
Six is the number **6**.
چھ

size *noun*
sizes
The **size** of something is how big or small it is.
سائز(قد)
*The **size** of the room is about five metres by seven metres.*

skate *noun*
skates
Skates are boots with a thin metal bar on the bottom for moving quickly on ice.
اسکیٹ، برف رانی کیلئے پیروں میں پہنا جانے والا تختہ

skeleton *noun*
skeletons
A **skeleton** is all the bones in a person's or animal's body.
ہڈیوں کا ڈھانچہ
*A human **skeleton** has more than 200 bones.*

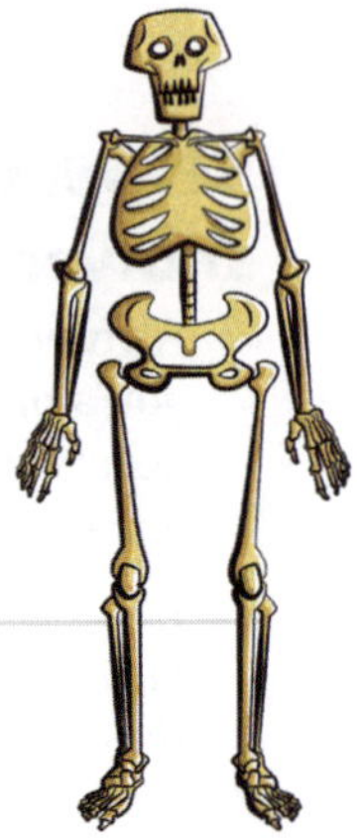

skies
⇨ Look at **sky**.
*The **skies** were grey.*

skill *noun*

If you have **skill** you are able to do something well.

مہارت

*He shows great **skill** on the football field.*

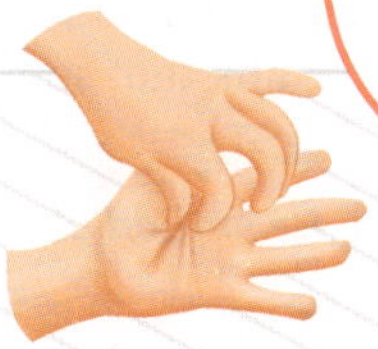

skin *noun*

skins

1 Your **skin** covers your whole body.

جلد، چمڑی

*Too much sun can damage your **skin**.*

2 The **skin** of a fruit or vegetable covers the outside of it.

چھلکا

*She slipped on a banana **skin**.*

skip *verb*

skips, skipping, skipped

1 If you **skip** along, you move along jumping from one foot to the other.

کودنا، اچھلنا

*We **skipped** down the street.*

2 If you **skip** something, you decide not to do it.

چھوڑ دینا

*Don't **skip** breakfast.*

skirt *noun*

skirts

A **skirt** is something that women and girls wear. It hangs down from the waist and covers part of the legs.

اِسکرٹ (لہنگا)

skull *noun*

skulls

A person's or animal's **skull** is the bones of their head.

کھوپڑی

*Your **skull** protects your brain.*

sky *noun*

skies

The **sky** is the space around the Earth which you can see when you look up.

آسمان

*The sun was shining in the **sky**.*

sleep *verb*

sleeps, sleeping, slept

If you **sleep**, you rest with your eyes closed and you do not move.

نیند

*Be quiet! The baby is **sleeping**.*

sleeve *noun*

sleeves

The **sleeves** of something you wear are the parts that cover your arms.

آستین

*She wore a blue dress with long **sleeves**.*

slept

⇨ Look at **sleep**.

*She **slept** for three hours.*

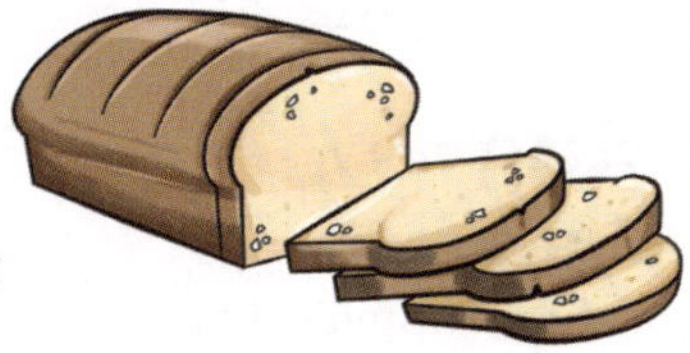

slice *noun*

slices

A **slice** of something is a thin piece that you cut from a larger piece.

ٹکڑا، قتلہ

*Would you like a **slice** of bread?*

slide *verb*

slides, sliding, slid

When someone or something **slides**, they move quickly over a surface.

پھسلنا

*She **slid** across the ice on her stomach.*

slip *verb*

slips, slipping, slipped

If you **slip**, you slide and fall.

پھسل جانا

*He **slipped** on the wet grass.*

slipper *noun*

slippers

Slippers are loose, soft shoes that you wear indoors.

چپل

*She put on a pair of **slippers**.*

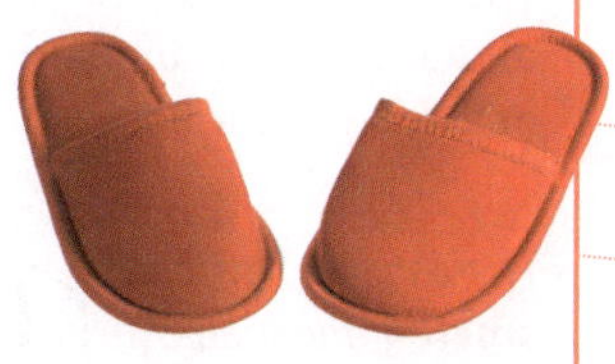

slippery *adjective*

If something is **slippery**, it is smooth or wet, and is difficult to walk on or to hold.

پھسلن بھرا

*Be careful—the floor is **slippery**.*

slope *noun*

slopes

A **slope** is the side of a mountain, hill, or valley.

ڈھلان

*A steep **slope** leads to the beach.*

slow *adjective*

slower, slowest

If something is **slow**, it does not move quickly.

سست

*The bus was very **slow**.*

slowly

If something moves **slowly**, it does not move quickly.

دھیرے دھیرے، آہستگی سے

slug *noun*

slugs

A **slug** is a small animal with a long soft body and no legs that moves very slowly.

گھونگھا

small *adjective*

smaller, smallest

If something is **small**, it is not large in size or amount.

چھوٹا

*She is **small** for her age.*

smash *verb*

smashes, smashing, smashed

If you **smash** something, it breaks into many pieces.

ٹکڑے کر ڈالنا

*The plate **smashed** when it hit the floor.*

smell *noun*

smells

The **smell** of something is what you notice about it when you breathe in through your nose.

بو

*There was a horrible **smell** in the fridge.*

smile *verb*

smiles, smiling, smiled

If you **smile**, the corners of your mouth turn up because you are happy or you think that something is funny.

مسکراہٹ

*He **smiled** at me.*

smoke *noun*

Smoke is the black or white clouds of gas that you see in the air when something burns.

دھواں

*Thick black **smoke** blew over the city.*

smooth *adjective*

smoother, smoothest

Something **smooth** has no rough parts, lumps, or holes.

ہموار، چکنا

*The baby's skin was soft and **smooth**.*

snail *noun*

snails

A **snail** is a small animal with a long, soft body, no legs, and a round shell on its back.

گھونگا

snake *noun*

snakes

A **snake** is a long, thin animal with no legs, that slides along the ground.

سانپ

sneeze *verb*

sneezes, sneezing, sneezed

When you **sneeze**, you suddenly take in air and then blow it down your nose in a noisy way.

چھینکنا

*Cover your nose and mouth when you **sneeze**.*

snow *noun*

Snow is pieces of soft white frozen water that fall from the sky.

برف باری، برف

*Six inches of **snow** fell last night.*

soap *noun*

Soap is something that you use with water for washing yourself.

صابن

*She bought a bar of **soap**.*

sock *noun*

socks

Socks are pieces of cloth that you wear over your foot and ankle, inside your shoes.

موزہ

*I have a pair of red **socks**.*

sofa *noun*

sofas

A **sofa** is a long, comfortable seat with a back, that two or three people can sit on.

صوفہ

soft *adjective*

softer, softest

1 Something that is **soft** is nice to touch, and not rough or hard.

ملائم، نرم

*She wiped the baby's face with a **soft** cloth.*

2 A **soft** sound or light is very gentle.

نرم، ہلکی

*There was a **soft** tapping on my door.*

soil *noun*

Soil is the top layer on the surface of the earth in which plants grow.

مٹی

*The **soil** here is good for growing vegetables.*

sold

⇨ Look at **sell**.

*They **sold** their house today.*

soldier *noun*

soldiers

A **soldier** is someone who is in an army.

سپاہی

solid *adjective*

1 Something that is **solid** stays the same shape if it is in a container or not.

ٹھوس

2 Something that is **solid** is not hollow.

سخت، ٹھوس

*They had to cut through 5 feet of **solid** rock.*

some

You use **some** to talk about an amount of something.

کچھ، تھوڑا

*Can I have **some** orange juice please?*

somebody

You use **somebody** to talk about a person without saying who you mean.

کوئی شخص

someone

You use **someone** to talk about a person without saying who you mean.

کوئی

*I need **someone** to help me.*

something

You use **something** to talk about a thing without saying what it is.

کوئی چیز (کچھ چیز)

*He knew that there was **something** wrong.*

sometimes

You use **sometimes** to talk about things that do not take place all the time.

کبھی بھی (آنے والے وقت میں)

***Sometimes** he's a little rude.*

a b c d e f g h i j k l m n o p q r s t u v w x y z

A B C D E F G H I J K L M N O P Q R S T U V W X Y Z

somewhere

You use **somewhere** to talk about a place without saying where you mean.

کسی جگہ

I've seen him before ***somewhere****.*

son *noun*

sons

Someone's **son** is their male child.

بیٹا

His ***son*** *is seven years old.*

song *noun*

songs

A **song** is words and music sung together.

گیت

She sang a ***song****.*

soon *adjective*

sooner, soonest

If you are going to do something **soon** you will do it a very short time from now.

جلد

I'll call you ***soon****.*

sore *adjective*

sorer, sorest

If part of your body is **sore**, it is painful.

خراش، چھالہ

I had a ***sore*** *throat.*

sorry *adjective*

sorrier, sorriest

1 If you are **sorry** about something, you feel sad about it.
معذرت خواہی، افسوس ہونا
I'm ***sorry*** *he's gone.*

2 If you feel **sorry** for someone, you feel sad for them.
دکھ محسوس کرنا، غمزدہ ہونا
I felt ***sorry*** *for him because nobody listened to him.*

sort *noun*

sorts

The different **sorts** of something are the different types of it.

قسم

What ***sort*** *of school do you go to?*

sound *noun*

sounds

A **sound** is something that you hear.

آواز

He heard the ***sound*** *of a car engine outside.*

soup *noun*

Soup is liquid food made by boiling meat, fish, or vegetables in water.

شوربہ

sour *adjective*

Something that is **sour** has a sharp, nasty taste.

کھٹا

Lemons have a ***sour*** *taste.*

south *noun*

The **south** is the direction to your right when you are looking towards the place where the sun rises.

جنوب

space *noun*

spaces

1 You use **space** to talk about an area that is empty.
خالی جگہ
They cut down trees to make ***space*** *for houses.*

2 **Space** is the area past the Earth, where the stars and planets are.
خلاء
The six astronauts will spend ten days in ***space****.*

spade *noun*

spades

A **spade** is a tool that is used for digging.

پھاوڑا

speak *verb*

speaks, speaking, spoken

When you **speak**, you say words.

بولنا

He ***spoke*** *in a whisper.*

special *adjective*

Someone or something that is **special** is better or more important than other people or things.

خاص

*Mum made a **special** cake for my birthday.*

speed *noun*

speeds

The **speed** of something is how fast it moves or is done.

رفتار

*He drove off at high **speed**.*

spell *verb*

spells, spelling, spelled or **spelt**

When you **spell** a word, you write or say each letter in the correct order.

ہجے کرنا

*He **spelled** his name.*

spend *verb*

spends, spending, spent

1 When you **spend** money, you buy things with it.

خرچ کرنا

*I have **spent** all my money.*

2 To **spend** time or energy is to use it doing something.

گزارنا

*She **spends** hours working on her garden.*

spider *noun*

spiders

A **spider** is a small animal with eight legs.

مکڑی

spill *verb*

spills, spilling, spilled or **spilt**

If you **spill** a liquid, you make it flow over the edge of a container by accident.

چھلک جانا

*He always **spilled** the drinks.*

spin *verb*

spins, spinning, spun

If something **spins**, it turns around quickly.

گردش کرنا، گھومنا

*He made the coin **spin** on his desk.*

spine *noun*

spines

Your **spine** is the row of bones down your back.

ریڑھ کی ہڈی کا منکا

splash *verb*

splashes, splashing, splashed

If you **splash** in water, you hit the water in a noisy way.

پانی کے چھینٹے اڑانا

*The children **splashed** around in the water.*

spoil *verb*

spoils, spoiling, spoiled or **spoilt**

1 If you **spoil** something, you damage it or stop it from working as it should.

برباد کرنا، روکنا، ختم کرنا

*Don't **spoil** the surprise.*

2 If you **spoil** children, you give them everything they want or ask for.

بگاڑنا

*She acted like a **spoilt** child.*

spoke *noun*
spokes

The **spokes** of a wheel are the bars which join the outside ring to the centre.

اسپوک، تیلی

spoke
➯ Look at **speak**.

*She **spoke** in a loud voice.*

spoken
➯ Look at **speak**.

*He has **spoken** to us.*

spoon *noun*
spoons

A **spoon** is a long tool with a round end that is used for eating, serving or mixing food.

چمچ

*He stirred his coffee with a **spoon**.*

sport *noun*
sports

Sports are games which need energy and skill.

کھیل

*She is very good at **sport**.*

spot *noun*
spots

Spots are small, round areas on a surface.

دھبہ، داغ

*The leaves are yellow with orange **spots**.*

spot *verb*
spots, spotting, spotted

If you **spot** something or someone, you notice them.

نشاندہی کرنا

*I didn't **spot** the mistake in his work.*

spout *noun*
spouts

A **spout** is a tube for pouring liquid.

ٹونٹی، نلی

*My kettle has a long **spout**.*

spray *noun*
sprays

Spray is a lot of small drops of water that are thrown into the air.

چھڑکاؤ

*The **spray** from the waves covered them.*

spread *verb*
spreads, spreading, spread

1 If you **spread** something somewhere, you open it out.
پھیلانا
*She **spread** a towel on the sand and lay on it.*

2 If you **spread** something on a surface, you put it all over the surface.
پھیلانا
*She was **spreading** butter on the bread.*

3 If something **spreads**, it reaches a larger area.
پھیلنا
*The news **spread** quickly.*

spring *noun*
springs

1 **Spring** is the season between winter and summer when the weather becomes warmer and plants start to grow again.
موسم بہار
*They are getting married next **spring**.*

2 A **spring** is a long piece of metal that goes round and round. It goes back to the same shape after you pull it.
اسپرنگ
*The **springs** in the bed were old.*

spun
➯ Look at **spin**.

*He **spun** the wheel.*

square *noun*
squares

A **square** is a shape with four straight sides that are all the same length.

مربع نما شکل

*Cut the cake in **squares**.*

squirrel *noun*
squirrels

A **squirrel** is a small animal with a long thick tail. **Squirrels** live in trees.

گلہری

stable *noun*
stables

A **stable** is a building where people keep horses.

اصطبل

stairs *noun*

Stairs are steps you walk down or up in a building.

سیڑھیاں

*He walked up the **stairs**.*

stamp *noun*
stamps

A **stamp** is a small piece of paper that you stick on an envelope before you post it.

ٹکٹ

*She put a **stamp** on the corner of the envelope.*

stamp *verb*
stamps, stamping, stamped

If you **stamp** your foot, you put your foot down very hard on the ground.

پٹخنا

*I **stamped** my feet to keep warm.*

stand *verb*
stands, standing, stood

When you are **standing**, you are on your feet.

کھڑے ہونا

*She was **standing** beside my bed.*

star *noun*
stars

1 A **star** is a large ball of burning gas in space. **Stars** look like small points of light in the sky.
ستارہ، تارے
***Stars** lit the sky.*

2 A **star** is a shape that has four, five, or more points sticking out of it in a pattern.
ستارہ
*How many **stars** are there on the flag?*

3 A **star** is somebody who is famous for doing something, for example acting or singing.
اسٹار، مقبول شخص
*He's one of the **stars** of a TV show.*

start *verb*
starts, starting, started

1 When something **starts**, it begins.
آغاز ہونا، شروع ہونا
*When does the film **start**?*

2 If you **start** to do something, you begin to do it.
شروع کرنا
*She **started** to read her book.*

station *noun*
stations

A **station** is a place where trains or buses stop so that people can get on or off.

اِسٹیشن

*We went to the train **station**.*

stay *verb*
stays, staying, stayed

1 If you **stay** in a place, you do not move away from it.
ٹھہرنا، برقرار رہنا
*She **stayed** in bed until noon.*

2 If you **stay** somewhere, you live there for a short time.
قیام کرنا، ٹھہرنا
*He **stayed** with them for two weeks.*

steady *adjective*
steadier, steadiest

Something that is **steady** is firm and not shaking.

مضبوط

*He held out a **steady** hand.*

steal *verb*
steals, stealing, stole, stolen

If you **steal** something from someone, you take it without asking or telling them and don't give it back.

چرانا

*They said he **stole** a bicycle.*

steam *noun*

Steam is the hot gas that water becomes when it boils.

بھاپ

*The **steam** rose into the air.*

steel *noun*

Steel is a very strong metal that is made from iron.

فولاد

*The door is made of **steel**.*

steep *adjective*

steeper, steepest

A **steep** slope rises quickly and is difficult to go up.

ڈھلوان

*Some of the hills are very **steep**.*

stem *noun*

stems

The **stem** of a plant is the long, thin part that the flowers and leaves grow on.

تنا

*He cut the **stem** and gave her the flower.*

step *noun*

steps

1 If you take a **step**, you lift your foot and put it down in a different place.
قدم
*I took a **step** towards him.*

2 A **step** is a flat surface that you put your feet on to walk up or down to somewhere.
سیڑھی
*We went down the **steps** into the garden.*

stick *noun*

sticks

A **stick** is a long, thin piece of wood.

تیلیاں، ٹہنی

*She put some dry **sticks** on the fire.*

stick *verb*

sticks, sticking, stuck

If you **stick** one thing to another, you join them together using glue.

چپکنا، چپکانا

*Now **stick** your picture on a piece of paper.*

stiff *adjective*

stiffer, stiffest

Something that is **stiff** is firm and is not easy to bend.

سخت، بے لچک

*The sheet of cardboard was **stiff**.*

still *adjective*

stiller, stillest

If you are **still**, you are not moving.

بلا حرکت، جامد

*Please stand **still**.*

sting *verb*

stings, stinging, stung

If a plant, an animal, or an insect **stings** you, a part of it is pushed into your skin so that you feel a sharp pain.

ڈنک مارنا

*She was **stung** by a bee.*

stir *verb*

stirs, stirring, stirred

When you **stir** a liquid, you move it around using a spoon or a stick.

تحریک پیدا کرنا، ہلانا

stole

⇨ Look at **steal**.

*They **stole** our car last night.*

stolen

⇨ Look at **steal**.

*All of her money was **stolen**.*

stomach *noun*

stomachs

Your **stomach** is the place inside your body where food goes when you eat it.

پیٹ

*His **stomach** felt full after the meal.*

stone *noun*

stones

1 **Stone** is a hard solid material that is found in the ground. It is often used for building.

پتھر

*The floor was solid **stone**.*

2 A **stone** is a small piece of rock that is found on the ground.

کنکر

*He took a **stone** out of his shoe.*

stood

⇨ Look at **stand**.

*He **stood** in the street.*

stop *verb*

stops, stopping, stopped

1 If you **stop** doing something, you do not do it any more.

روکنا

***Stop** throwing those stones!*

2 If something **stops**, it does not do what it did any more.

رکنا، ٹھہرجانا

*The rain has **stopped**.*

store *verb*

stores, storing, stored

If you **store** something, you keep it somewhere safe.

محفوظ کرنا، ذخیرہ کرنا

storm *noun*

storms

A **storm** is very bad weather, with heavy rain and strong winds.

طوفان

*There will be **storms** along the East Coast.*

story *noun*

stories

When someone tells you a **story** they describe people and things that are not real, in a way that makes you enjoy hearing about them.

داستان

*I'm going to tell you a **story** about four little rabbits.*

straight *adjective*

straighter, straightest

If something is **straight**, it goes one way and does not bend.

سیدھی، راست

*The boat moved in a **straight** line.*

strange *adjective*

stranger, strangest

Something that is **strange** is unusual.

عجیب

*I had a **strange** dream last night.*

straw *noun*

straws

1 **Straw** is the dry, yellow stems of crops.

تنکا

*The floor of the barn was covered with **straw**.*

2 A **straw** is a thin tube that you use to suck a drink into your mouth.

اسٹرا، نلکی

*I drank my milk through a **straw**.*

strawberry *noun*

strawberries

A **strawberry** is a small soft red fruit that has a lot of very small seeds on its skin.

اسٹرابیری

stream *noun*

streams

A **stream** is a small narrow river.

دھارا، چھوٹا دریا

*There was a **stream** at the end of the garden.*

A B C D E F G H I J K L M N O P Q R S T U V W X Y Z

street *noun*

streets

A **street** is a road in a city or a town.

گلی، گلیارا

*The **streets** were full of people.*

strength *noun*

Your **strength** is how strong you are.

طاقت

*Swimming builds up the **strength** of your muscles.*

stretch *verb*

stretches, stretching, stretched

1 Something that **stretches** over an area covers all of it.

پھیلنا

*The line of cars **stretched** for miles.*

2 When you **stretch**, you hold out part of your body as far as you can.

پھیلانا

*He yawned and **stretched**.*

strict *adjective*

stricter, strictest

A **strict** person expects people to obey rules.

سخت

*My parents are very **strict**.*

string *noun*

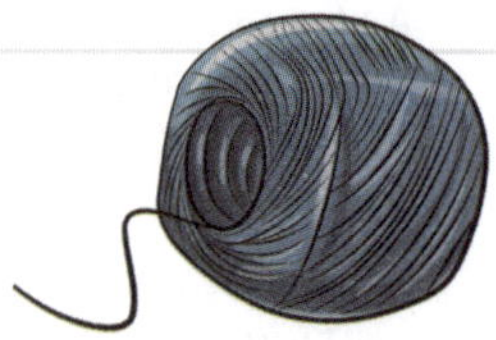

strings

1 **String** is thin rope that is made of twisted threads.

رسی

*He held out a small bag tied with **string**.*

2 The **strings** on an instrument are the thin pieces of wire that are stretched across it and that make sounds when the instrument is played.

تار

*He changed a guitar **string**.*

strip *noun*

strips

A **strip** of something is a long, narrow piece of it.

پٹی

*Cut a **strip** off a piece of paper, then twist it and stick the two ends together. Then cut it along the middle and see what happens.*

stripe *noun*

stripes

A **stripe** is a long line that is a different colour from the areas next to it.

دھاری، پٹی

*She wore a blue skirt with white **stripes**.*

strong *adjective*

stronger, strongest

1 Someone who is **strong** is healthy with good muscles.

طاقتور

*I'm not **strong** enough to carry him.*

2 **Strong** things are not easy to break.

مضبوط

*This **strong** plastic will not crack.*

stuck *adjective*

1 If something is **stuck** in a place, it cannot move.

پھنسا ہوا

*His car got **stuck** in the snow.*

2 If you get **stuck**, you can't go on doing something because it is too difficult.

رکا ہوا

*The teacher will help if you get **stuck**.*

stung

⇨ Look at **sting**.

*He was **stung** by a wasp.*

submarine *noun*

submarines

A **submarine** is a ship that can travel under the sea.

آبدوز

subtraction *noun*

Subtraction is when you take one number away from another.

گھٹاؤ

suck *verb*

sucks, sucking, sucked

If you **suck** something, you hold it in your mouth for a long time.

چوسنا

*They **sucked** their sweets.*

sudden *adjective*

Something **sudden** is quick and is not expected.

اچانک

*The car came to a **sudden** stop.*

suddenly

Suddenly is quickly, without being expected.

اچانک

***Suddenly** there was a loud bang.*

sugar *noun*

Sugar is a sweet thing that is used for making food and drinks taste sweet.

شکر

*Do you take **sugar** in your coffee?*

suit *noun*

suits

A **suit** is a jacket and trousers or a skirt that are made from the same cloth.

سوٹ (کوٹ پینٹ جیکیٹ)

*He was wearing a dark **suit**.*

sum *noun*

sums

1 A **sum** of money is an amount of money.

رقم، مقدار

*Large **sums** of money were lost.*

2 In maths, a **sum** is a problem you work out using numbers.

جوڑ، مثبت

*I have to finish these **sums**.*

summer *noun*

summers

Summer is the season after spring and before autumn. In the **summer** the weather is usually warm or hot.

موسم گرما

sun *noun*

suns

The **sun** is the large ball of burning gas in the sky that gives us light.

سورج

*The **sun** was now high in the sky.*

Sunday *noun*

Sundays

Sunday is the day after Saturday and before Monday.

اتوار

*We went for a drive on **Sunday**.*

sunflower *noun*

sunflowers

A **sunflower** is a very tall plant with large yellow flowers.

اتوار

sung

Look at **sing**.

*She has **sung** the song many times before.*

sunk

Look at **sink**.

*The rock has **sunk** to the bottom of the river.*

sunny *adjective*

sunnier, sunniest

When it is **sunny**, the sun is shining.

دھوپ دار

*The weather was warm and **sunny**.*

sunshine *noun*

Sunshine is the light that comes from the sun.

سورج کی دھوپ اور گرمی

*She was sitting outside in bright **sunshine**.*

supermarket *noun*

supermarkets

A **supermarket** is a large shop that sells all kinds of food and other things for the home.

سبھی سامان کی دوکان

*Lots of people buy food in a **supermarket**.*

sure *adjective*

If you are **sure** that something is true, you know that it is true.

یقینی

*I am **sure** my answer is correct.*

surface *noun*

surfaces

The **surface** of something is the flat top part of it or the outside of it.

سطح

*There were pen marks on the table's **surface**.*

surname *noun*

surnames

Your **surname** is your last name which you share with other people in your family.

خاندانی نام

surprise *noun*

surprises

A **surprise** is something that you do not expect.

حیرت

*I have a **surprise** for you!*

swallow *verb*

swallows, swallowing, swallowed

If you **swallow** something, you make it go from your mouth down into your stomach.

نگلنا

*She took a bite of the apple and **swallowed** it.*

swam

⇨ Look at **swim**.

*She **swam** across the river.*

swan *noun*

swans

A **swan** is a large bird with a long neck, that lives on rivers and lakes.

ہنس

sweep *verb*

sweeps, sweeping, swept

If you **sweep** an area, you push dirt off it using a brush with a long handle.

پونچھنا

*The man in the shop was **sweeping** the floor.*

sweet *adjective*

sweeter, sweetest

Sweet food and drink has a lot of sugar in it.

میٹھا

*Mum gave me a cup of **sweet** tea.*

sweet *noun*

sweets

Sweets are foods that have a lot of sugar.

مٹھائی

*Don't eat too many **sweets**.*

swept

⇨ Look at **swept**.

*The rubbish was **swept** away.*

swim *verb*

swims, swimming, swam, swum

When you **swim**, you move through water by moving your arms and legs.

تیرنا

*She learned to **swim** when she was three.*

swing *verb*

swings, swinging, swung

If something **swings**, it keeps moving backwards and forwards or from side to side through the air.

جھلانا، گھمانا

*She walked beside him with her arms **swinging**.*

switch *noun*

switches

A **switch** is a small button for turning something on or off.

سوئچ، بٹن

*She pressed the **switch** to turn on the light.*

sword *noun*

swords

A **sword** is like a long knife, with a handle and a long sharp blade.

تلوار

swum

⇨ Look at **swim**.

*He had never **swum** so far.*

swung

⇨ Look at **swing**.

*She **swung** her bag backwards and forwards.*

Tt

table *noun*

tables

A **table** is a piece of furniture that has legs and a flat top.

میز، ٹیبل

tadpole *noun*

tadpoles

A **tadpole** is a small black animal with a round head and a long tail that lives in water. **Tadpoles** grow into frogs or toads.

مینڈک کا بچہ

tail *noun*

tails

An animal's **tail** is the long, thin part at the end of its body.

دم

take *verb*

takes, taking, took, taken

1 If you **take** something, you move it or carry it.
لینا
*She **took** the plates into the kitchen.*

2 If you **take** something that does not belong to you, you steal it.
لینا
*Someone **took** all our money.*

3 If you **take** a vehicle, you ride in it from one place to another.
پکڑنا، سوار ہونا
*We **took** the bus to school.*

talk *verb*

talks, talking, talked

When you **talk**, you say things to someone.

بات کرنا

*She **talked** to him on the phone.*

a b c d e f g h i j k l m n o p q r s t u v w x y z

A B C D E F G H I J K L M N O P Q R S T U V W X Y Z

tall *adjective*
taller, tallest
If a person or thing is **tall**, they are higher than usual from top to bottom.
لمبا
*It was a very **tall** building.*

tame *adjective*
tamer, tamest
If an animal or bird is **tame**, it is not afraid of people and will not try to hurt them.
پالتو، سدھایا ہوا

tap *verb*
taps, tapping, tapped
If you **tap** something, you hit it but you do not use a lot of strength.
کھٹکھٹانا
*He **tapped** on the door and went in.*

tape *noun*
Tape is a long, thin strip of plastic that has glue on one side. You use **tape** to stick things together.
ٹیپ لگانا
*He wrapped the parcel with paper and **tape**.*

taste *verb*
tastes, tasting, tasted
If you **taste** something, you eat or drink a small amount of it to see what it is like.
ذائقہ لینا، چکھنا
*She **tasted** the soup and then added some salt.*

taught
⇨ Look at **teach**.
*My mum **taught** me to read.*

tea *noun*
1 **Tea** is a drink. You make it by pouring hot water on to the dry leaves of a plant called the **tea** bush.
چائے

2 **Tea** is also a meal that you eat in the afternoon or the early evening.
ہلکے ناشتے کے ساتھ چائے

teach *verb*
teaches, teaching, taught
If you **teach** someone something, you help them to understand it or you show them how to do it.
پڑھانا
*He **teaches** people how to play the piano.*

teacher *noun*
teachers
A **teacher** is a person whose job is to teach other people. **Teachers** usually work in schools.
استاد

team *noun*
teams
A **team** is a group of people who work together, or who play a sport together against another group.
گروہ، دستہ، ٹیم
*He is in the school football **team**.*

tear *noun*
tears
Tears are the liquid that comes out of your eyes when you cry.
آنسو
*Her face was wet with **tears**.*

tear *verb*
tears, tearing, tore, torn
If you **tear** something, you pull it into pieces or make a hole in it.
پھاڑنا
*Try not to **tear** the paper.*

teeth

⇨ Look at **tooth**.

*Clean your **teeth** before you go to bed.*

telephone *noun*

telephones

A **telephone** is a machine that you use to talk to someone who is in another place.

ٹیلیفون

television *noun*

televisions

A **television** is a machine that shows moving pictures with sound on a screen.

ٹیلیویژن

tell *verb*

tells, telling, told

1 If you **tell** someone something, you let them know about it.
بتانا، کہنا
__Tell__ me about your holiday.

2 If you **tell** someone to do something, you say that they must do it.
کہنا
She __told__ me to go away.

3 If you can **tell** something, you know it.
بتانا
I can __tell__ that he is angry.

ten *noun*

Ten is the number **10**.

دس

tent *noun*

tents

A **tent** is made of strong material that is held up with long pieces of metal and ropes. You sleep in a **tent** when you stay in a camp.

خیمہ، تنبو

term *noun*

terms

A **term** is one of the parts of a school year. There are usually three **terms** in a year.

تعلیمی دورانیہ، تعلیمی میعاد، وقفہ

terrible *adjective*

If something is **terrible**, it is very bad.

خوفناک، انتہائی خراب

That was a __terrible__ film.

test *verb*

tests, testing, tested

If you **test** something, you try it to see what it is like, or how it works.

جانچنا

__Test__ the water to see if it is warm.

test *noun*

tests

A **test** is something you do to show how much you know or what you can do.

ٹیسٹ، امتحان

The teacher gave us a maths __test__.

thank *verb*

thanks, thanking, thanked

When you **thank** someone, you tell them that you are pleased about something they have given you or have done for you. You usually do this by saying "Thank you".

شکریہ ادا کرنا

I __thanked__ him for my present.

theatre *noun*

theatres

A **theatre** is a building where you go to see people acting stories, singing, or dancing.

تھیٹر

their

You use **their** to say that something belongs to a group of people, animals, or things.

ان کا

*They took off **their** coats.*

theirs

You use **theirs** to say that something belongs to a group of people, animals, or things.

ان کی

*The house next to **theirs** was empty.*

then

1 **Then** means at that time.

کے مقابلے

*He wasn't as rich **then** as he is now.*

2 You also use **then** to say that one thing happens after another.

پھر

*She said good night, **then** went to bed.*

there

1 You use **there** to say that something is in a place or is happening, or to make someone notice it.

وہاں

***There** are flowers on the table.*

2 **There** also means to a place, or at a place.

وہاں

*I have never been **there** before.*

there's

There's is short for **there is**.

وہاں ہے

***There's** nothing in the box.*

they

You use **they** when you are talking about more than one person, animal, or thing.

وہ لوگ

***They** are all in the same class.*

they'd

1 **They'd** is short for **they had**.

انہوں نے کیا (ماضی)

2 **They'd** is also short for **they would**.

وہ کریں گے

*The boys said **they'd** come back later.*

they'll

They'll is short for **they will**.

وہ کریں گے

***They'll** be here on Monday.*

they're

They're is short for **they are**.

وہ کر رہے ہیں

***They're** going to the circus.*

they've

They've is short for **they have**.

وہ کر چکے ہیں

***They've** gone away.*

thick *adjective*

thicker, thickest

1 If something is **thick**, it is deep or wide between one side and the other.

موٹا

*He cut a **thick** slice of bread.*

2 If a liquid is **thick**, it flows slowly.

گاڑھا

*This soup is very **thick**.*

thigh *noun*

thighs

Your **thighs** are the parts of your legs that are above your knees.

جانگھ

*His **thighs** ached from climbing the hill.*

thin *adjective*

thinner, thinnest

1 If something is **thin**, it is narrow between one side and the other.

پتلا

*The book is printed on very **thin** paper.*

2 If a person or animal is **thin**, they are not fat and they do not weigh much.

دبلا

*He was a tall, **thin** man.*

thing *noun*
things
A **thing** is something that is not a plant, an animal, or a human being.

چیز

*What's that **thing** lying in the road?*

think *verb*
thinks, thinking, thought
1. If you **think** something, you believe that it is true.

   سوچنا

   *I **think** it's a great idea.*
2. When you **think**, you use your mind.

   سوچنا، غور کرنا

   *I tried to **think** what to do.*

thirsty *adjective*
thirstier, thirstiest
If you are **thirsty**, you want to drink something.

پیاسا

thought
⇨ Look at **think**.

*I **thought** they were here.*

thread *noun*
threads
Thread is a long, thin piece of cotton or wool that you use to sew cloth.

دھاگا

three *noun*
Three is the number **3**.

تین

threw
⇨ Look at **throw**.

*She **threw** her coat on to a chair.*

throat *noun*
throats
1. Your **throat** is the back part of your mouth that you use to swallow and to breathe.

   حلق
2. Your **throat** is also the front part of your neck.

   گلا

through
Through means going all the way from one side of something to the other side.

اوّل تا آخر

*We walked **through** the forest.*

throw *verb*
throws, throwing, threw, thrown
When you **throw** something you are holding, you move your hand quickly and let the thing go, so that it moves through the air.

پھینکنا

***Throw** the ball to me.*

thumb *noun*
thumbs
Your **thumb** is the short, thick finger on the side of your hand.

انگوٹھا

*The baby sucked its **thumb**.*

thunder *noun*
Thunder is the loud noise that you sometimes hear from the sky when there is a storm.

گرج، گھن گرج

Thursday *noun*
Thursdays
Thursday is the day after Wednesday and before Friday.

جمعرات

*I saw her on **Thursday**.*

A B C D E F G H I J K L M N O P Q R S T U V W X Y Z

tidy *adjective*
tidier, tidiest
Something that is **tidy** is neat, with everything in its proper place.
صاف ستھرا

tie *verb*
ties, tying, tied
If you **tie** something, you fasten it with string or a rope.
باندھنا
*He **tied** the dog to the fence.*

tie *noun*
ties
A **tie** is a long, narrow piece of cloth that you tie a knot in and wear around your neck with a shirt.
ٹائی

tiger *noun*
tigers
A **tiger** is a large wild cat that has orange fur with black stripes.
شیر

tight *adjective*
tighter, tightest
1 If clothes are **tight**, they are so small that they fit very close to your body.
تنگ
*His trousers were very **tight**.*
2 Something that is **tight** is fastened so that it is not easy to move it.
سخت
*The string was tied in a **tight** knot.*

time *noun*
1 **Time** is how long something takes to happen. We measure **time** in minutes, hours, days, weeks, months, and years.
وقت
*I've known him for a long **time**.*
2 The **time** is a moment in the day that you describe in hours and minutes.
وقت
*"What **time** is it?"—"Ten past five."*

tin *noun*
tins
1 **Tin** is a kind of soft, pale grey metal.
ٹن
2 A **tin** is a metal container for food.
ٹن، ڈبا
*She opened a **tin** of beans.*

tiny *adjective*
tinier, tiniest
If something is **tiny**, it is very small.
چھوٹا سا
*Our new kitten is **tiny**.*

tired *adjective*
If you are **tired**, you need to rest or get some sleep.
تھکا ہوا

toad *noun*
toads
A **toad** is a small animal that looks like a frog. **Toads** have rough, dry skin and live on land.
مینڈک کی ایک قسم

today
Today means the day that is happening now.
آج
*I feel much better **today**.*

toe *noun*
toes
Your **toes** are the five parts at the end of each foot.
پیر کا پنجہ
*I'm sorry I stood on your **toes**.*

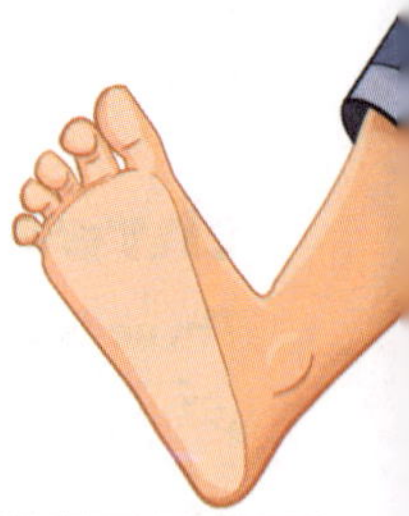

together
If people do something **together**, they do it with each other.
ساتھ ساتھ
*We played football **together**.*

told

⇨ Look at **tell**.

*We **told** them the answer.*

tomato *noun*

tomatoes

A **tomato** is a soft red fruit with a lot of juice.

ٹماٹر

tomorrow

Tomorrow is the day after today.

آنے والا کل

*I'll see you **tomorrow**.*

tongue *noun*

tongues

Your **tongue** is the soft part inside your mouth that moves when you eat or talk.

زبان

tonight

Tonight is the evening or night that will come at the end of today.

اِس رات کو، آج رات کو

*We're going out **tonight**.*

too

1. **Too** means also.

   بھی

   *Can I come **too**?*
2. You also use **too** to mean more than you want or need.

   کافی

   *The TV is **too** loud.*

took

⇨ Look at **take**.

*It **took** me hours.*

tool *noun*

tools

A **tool** is something that you hold in your hands and use to do a job.

آلہ

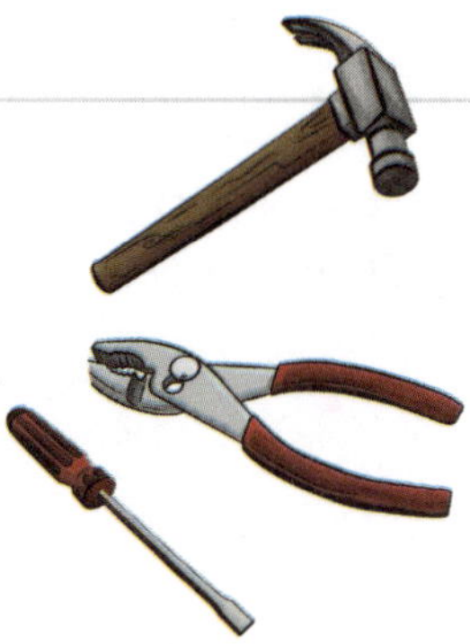

tooth *noun*

teeth

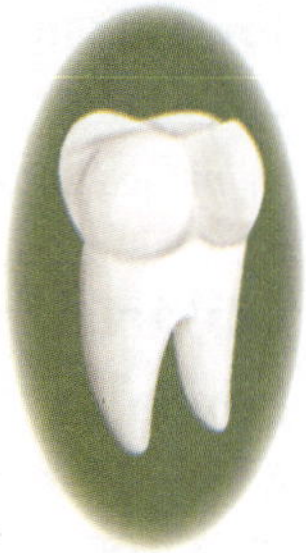

1. Your **teeth** are the hard, white things in your mouth that you use to bite and chew food.

   دانت

   *I clean my **teeth** twice a day.*
2. The **teeth** of a comb, a saw, or a zip are the parts that are in a row along its edge.

   دندانے

top *noun*

tops

1. The **top** of something is the highest part of it.

   چوٹی

   *We climbed to the **top** of the hill.*
2. The **top** of something is also the part that fits over the end of it.

   اوپری سرا، اوپر

   *He took the **top** off the jar.*

tore

⇨ Look at **tear**.

*She **tore** her dress on a nail.*

torn

⇨ Look at **tear**.

*He has **torn** the cover of the book.*

tortoise *noun*

tortoises

A **tortoise** is an animal with a hard shell on its back. It can pull its head and legs inside the shell. **Tortoises** move very slowly.

کچھوا

touch *verb*

touches, touching, touched

1. If you **touch** something, you put your fingers or your hand on it.

   چھوا

   *The baby **touched** my face.*
2. If one thing **touches** another, they are so close that there is no space between them.

   چھونا، پہنچنا

   *Her feet **touched** the floor.*

towards

Towards means in the direction of something.

طرف، جانب

*He moved **towards** the door.*

towel *noun*

towels

A **towel** is a piece of thick, soft cloth that you use to get yourself dry.

تولیہ

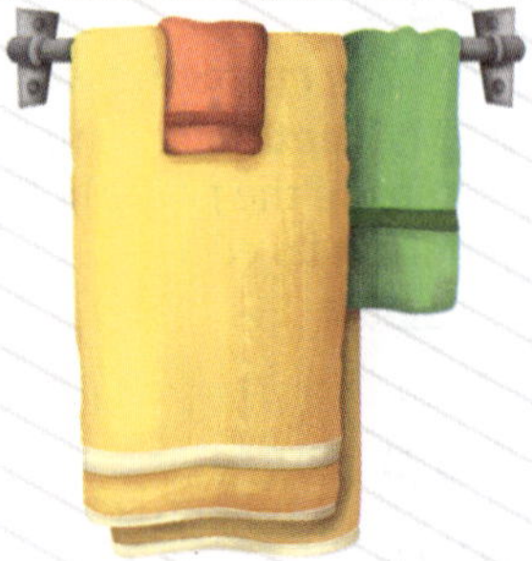

town *noun*

towns

A **town** is a place with a lot of streets, buildings, and shops, where people live and work.

شہر

toy *noun*

toys

A **toy** is something that you play with.

کھلونا

tractor *noun*

tractors

A **tractor** is a vehicle with big wheels at the back. **Tractors** are used on a farm to pull machines and other heavy things.

ٹریکٹر

traffic *noun*

Traffic is all the vehicles that are on a road at the same time.

ٹریفک (نقل و حمل)

*There is a lot of **traffic** in the town today.*

train *noun*

trains

A **train** is a long vehicle that is pulled by an engine along a railway line.

ٹرین، ریل گاڑی

travel *verb*

travels, travelling, travelled

When you **travel**, you go from one place to another.

سفر کرنا

*He **travelled** to many different countries.*

tree *noun*

trees

A **tree** is a very tall plant with branches, leaves, and a hard main part that is called a trunk.

درخت

triangle *noun*

triangles

1 A **triangle** is a shape with three straight sides.

مثلث

2 A **triangle** is also an instrument made of metal in the shape of a **triangle** that you hit with a stick to make music.

ٹرینگل (ساز)

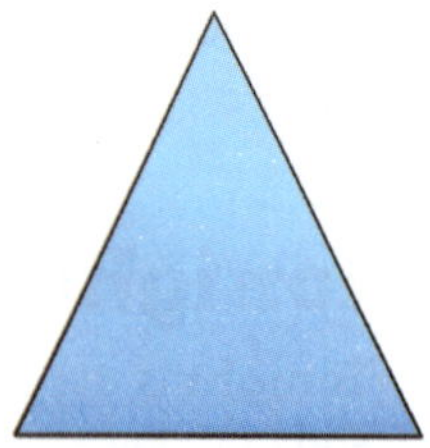

trick *verb*

tricks, tricking, tricked

If someone **tricks** you, they make you believe something that is not true so that you will do what they want.

ٹھگنا، دھوکہ دینا، فریب دینا

*They **tricked** her into giving them money.*

tried

⇨ Look at **try**.

*They **tried** their best.*

tries

⇨ Look at **try**.

*She **tries** to help.*

trip *noun*
trips
When you go on a **trip**, you travel to a place and then come back.
تفریحی سفر، پھیرا
*We went on a **trip** to the park.*

trousers *noun*
Trousers are things that you can wear. They cover the part of your body below the waist, and each leg.
پتلون
*He was wearing brown **trousers**.*

truck *noun*
trucks
A **truck** is a large vehicle that is used to carry things.
ٹرک

true *adjective*
1 If a story is **true**, it really happened.
درست، صحیح، سچ
*Everything she said was **true**.*
2 If something is **true**, it is right or correct.
سچ
*Is it **true** that you have six cats?*

trunk *noun*
trunks
1 A **trunk** is the thick stem of a tree. The branches and roots grow from the **trunk**.
تنا
2 An elephant's **trunk** is its long nose. Elephants use their **trunks** to suck up water and to lift things.
سونڈ
3 A **trunk** is also a large, strong box that you use to keep things in.
ٹرنک، صندوق

try *verb*
tries, trying, tried
1 If you **try** to do something, you do it as well as you can.
کوشش کرنا
*I will **try** to come tomorrow.*
2 If you **try** something, you test it to see what it is like or how it works.
آزمانا
*Would you like to **try** my new bike?*

tube *noun*
tubes
1 A **tube** is a long, round, hollow piece of metal, rubber, or plastic.
نلی
*The liquid goes through the **tube** into the bottle.*
2 A **tube** is also a soft metal or plastic container that you press to make what is in it come out.
ٹیوب
*He bought a **tube** of glue.*

Tuesday *noun*
Tuesdays
Tuesday is the day after Monday and before Wednesday.
منگل
*He came home on **Tuesday**.*

tune *noun*
tunes
A **tune** is a piece of music that is nice to listen to.
سر (موسیقی کا)
*She played a **tune** on the piano.*

tunnel *noun*
tunnels
A **tunnel** is a long hole that goes below the ground or through a hill.
سرنگ

A B C D E F G H I J K L M N O P Q R S T U V W X Y Z

turn *verb*
turns, turning, turned
1 When you **turn**, you move in a different direction.
واپس مڑنا
*He **turned** and walked away.*
2 When something **turns**, it moves around in a circle.
گھومنا
*The wheels **turned** slowly.*
3 If one thing **turns** into another thing, it becomes that thing.
تبدیل ہونا
*The tadpole **turned** into a frog.*
4 When you **turn** a machine on, you make it start working. When you **turn** it off, you make it stop working.
بند کرنا
*I **turned** off the television.*

tusk *noun*
tusks
An elephant's **tusks** are the two very long, curved teeth that it has beside its trunk.
سونڈ

TV *noun*
TVs
TV is short for **television**.
ٹیلی ویژن
*What's on **TV**?*

twelve *noun*
Twelve is the number **12**.
بارہ

twice
If something happens **twice**, it happens two times.
دوبار
*I've met him **twice**.*

twig *noun*
twigs
A **twig** is a very small, thin branch that grows on a tree or a bush.
ٹہنی

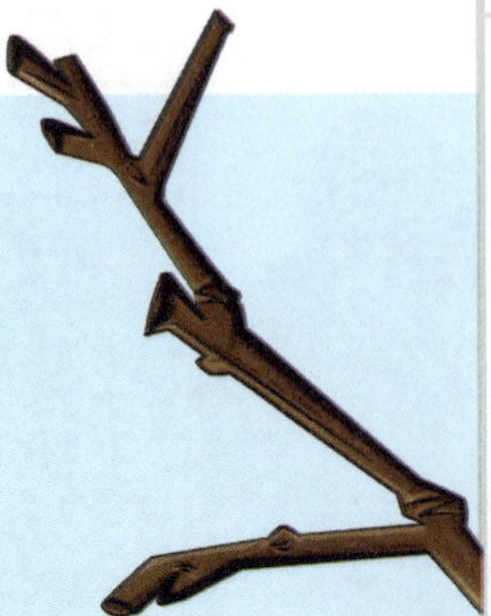

twin *noun*
twins
If two people are **twins**, they have the same parents and they were born on the same day. **Twins** often look alike.
جڑواں

twist *verb*
twists, twisting, twisted
If you **twist** something, you turn one end of it in one direction while you hold the other end or turn it in the opposite direction.
بٹنا، بل دینا
*She **twisted** the towel in her hands.*

two *noun*
Two is the number **2**.
دو

tying
⇨ Look at **tie**.
*He was **tying** the two pieces of rope together.*

type *noun*
types
A **type** of something is the kind of thing that it is.
قسم
*Owls are a **type** of bird.*

type *verb*
types, typing, typed
If you **type** something, you write it with a machine, for example a computer.
ٹائپ کرنا
*She **typed** a letter.*

tyre *noun*
tyres
A **tyre** is a thick circle made of strong rubber that goes round a wheel. **Tyres** usually have air inside them.
ٹائر (ہوا بھری ٹیوب کے ساتھ)

Uu

ugly *adjective*
uglier, ugliest

If something is **ugly**, it is not nice to look at.

بدشکل، بھدّا

*The monster had an **ugly** face.*

umbrella *noun*
umbrellas

An **umbrella** is a long stick that is joined to a cover made of cloth or plastic. You hold an **umbrella** over your head so that you will not get wet in the rain.

چھاتا

uncle *noun*
uncles

Your **uncle** is the brother of your mother or father, or the husband of your aunt.

چچا، ماموں

understand *verb*
understands, understanding, understood

If you **understand** something, you know what it means or why or how it happens.

سمجھنا

*I didn't **understand** what he said.*

underwear *noun*

Your **underwear** is the name for the clothes that you wear next to your skin, under all your other clothes.

انڈرویر

undress *verb*
undresses, undressing, undressed

When you **undress**, you take off your clothes.

کپڑے اتارنا

uniform *noun*
uniforms

A **uniform** is a special set of clothes that some people wear to show what job they do, or some children wear to show what school they go to.

وردی

*I put on my school **uniform**.*

until

If something happens **until** a time, it happens before that time and then stops at that time.

۔۔ ہونے تک

*Wait here **until** I come back.*

unusual *adjective*

If something is **unusual**, it does not happen very often.

غیر عادی

*It is **unusual** for him to be late.*

up

When something moves **up**, it moves from a lower place to a higher place.

اوپر

*She ran **up** the stairs.*

upon

Upon means the same as **on**.

پر، کے اوپر

*He stood **upon** the bridge.*

upset *adjective*

If you are **upset**, you are sad because something bad has happened.

پراگندہ

*I was **upset** when my brother broke my doll.*

upside down

1 If something is **upside down**, the part that is usually at the bottom is at the top.

الٹا

*The picture was **upside down**.*

2 If you hang **upside down**, your head is below your feet.

الٹا

urgent *adjective*

If something is **urgent**, it is very important and you need to do something about it quickly.

فوری توجہ کی حامل

*This problem is **urgent**.*

use *verb*

uses, using, used

If you **use** something, you do something with it.

استعمال کرنا

***Use** a cloth to clean the table.*

useful *adjective*

If something is **useful**, you can use it to do something or to help you in some way.

فائدہمند

usual *adjective*

Something that is **usual** is what happens most often.

معمول کا

*He arrived at his **usual** time.*

usually

If something **usually** happens, it is the thing that happens most often.

عام طور پر

*I **usually** take the bus to school.*

Vv

valley *noun*

valleys

A **valley** is a low area of land between hills.

وادی

valuable *adjective*

If something is **valuable**, it is worth a lot of money.

قیمتی سامان

van *noun*

vans

A **van** is a covered vehicle larger than a car but smaller than a lorry. People use **vans** for carrying things.

وین (موٹر گاڑی)

vase *noun*

vases

A **vase** is a jar for flowers.

گلدان

vegetable *noun*

vegetables

Vegetables are plants that you can cook and eat.

سبزی ترکاری

vehicle *noun*

vehicles

A **vehicle** is a machine that carries people or things from one place to another.

موٹر گاڑی

verb *noun*

verbs

A **verb** is a word like 'sing,' 'feel,' or 'eat' that you use for saying what someone or something does.

فعل

very

Very is used before a word to make it stronger.

بہت

*She had a **very** bad dream.*

vet *noun*

vets

A **vet** is a doctor for animals.

جانوروں کا ڈاکٹر، سلوتری

video *noun*

videos

A **video** is a copy of a film or television programme.

ویڈیو

village *noun*

villages

A **village** is a small town.

گاؤں

voice *noun*

voices

Your **voice** is the sound that comes from your mouth when you talk or sing.

آواز

volcano *noun*

volcanoes

A **volcano** is a mountain that throws out hot, liquid rock and fire.

آتش فشاں پہاڑ

vote *verb*

votes, voting, voted

When a group of people **vote**, everybody shows what they want to do, usually by writing on a piece of paper or by putting their hands up.

ووٹ کرنا

*We **voted** to send money to people who were in the earthquake.*

Ww

waist *noun*

waists

Your **waist** is the middle part of your body.

کمر

wait *verb*

waits, waiting, waited

When you **wait** for something or someone, you spend time doing very little, before something happens.

انتظار کرنا

wake *verb*

wakes, waking, woke, woken

When you **wake** up, you stop sleeping.

جاگنا، بیدار ہونا

walk *verb*

walks, walking, walked

When you **walk**, you move along by putting one foot in front of the other.

چلنا، ٹہلنا

wall *noun*

walls

A **wall** is one of the sides of a building or a room.

دیوار

want *verb*

wants, wanting, wanted

If you **want** something, you would like to have it.

چاہنا

a b c d e f g h i j k l m n o p q r s t u v w x y z

war *noun*
wars
A **war** is when countries or groups fight each other.
جنگ

wardrobe *noun*
wardrobes
A **wardrobe** is a tall cupboard that you can hang your clothes in.
کپڑوں کی آلماری

warm *adjective*
warmer, warmest
Something that is **warm** is not cold, but not hot.
گرم
*The bread is still **warm** from the oven.*

warn *verb*
warns, warning, warned
If you **warn** someone about a possible problem or danger, you tell them about it.
خبردار کرنا، آگاہ کرنا
*I **warned** them not to go.*

was
➩ Look at **be**.
*It **was** my birthday yesterday.*

wash *verb*
washes, washing, washed
If you **wash** something, you clean it using soap and water.
دھونا

wasn't
Wasn't is short for **was not**.
نہیں تھا
*She **wasn't** happy.*

wasp *noun*
wasps
A **wasp** is an insect with wings and yellow and black stripes across its body. **Wasps** can sting people.
بھڑ، بر

waste *verb*
wastes, wasting, wasted
If you **waste** time, money, or energy, you use too much of it on something that is not important.
کوڑا، قابل ضیاع چیز
*It's important not to **waste** water.*

watch *verb*
watches, watching, watched
If you **watch** something, you look at it for a period of time.
نگرانی کرنا، دیکھنا

watch *noun*
watches
A **watch** is a small clock that you wear on your wrist.
دستی گھڑی

water *noun*
Water is a clear liquid that has no colour, taste or smell. It falls from clouds as rain.
پانی

wave *noun*
waves
Waves on the surface of the sea are the parts that move up and down.
لہر
*The **waves** broke over the rocks.*

wave *verb*
waves, waving, waved
If you **wave** your hand, you move it from side to side, usually to say hello or goodbye.
ہاتھ ہلانا، الوداع کہنا

wax *noun*

Wax is a soft material that melts when you make it hot. It is used to make crayons and candles.

موم

way *noun*

ways

1 A **way** of doing something is how you do it.

طریقہ

*This is the **way** to throw the ball.*

2 The **way** to a place is how you get there.

راستہ

*We're going the wrong **way**!*

weak *adjective*

weaker, weakest

If someone or something is **weak**, they are not strong.

کمزور

*When she spoke, her voice was **weak**.*

wear *verb*

wears, wearing, wore, worn

When you **wear** clothes, shoes or glasses, you have them on your body.

پہننا

*What are you going to **wear** today?*

weather *noun*

The **weather** is what it is like outside, for example if it is raining or sunny.

موسم

*What will the **weather** be like tomorrow?*

web *noun*

webs

1 The **Web** is made up of a very large number of websites all joined together. You can use it anywhere in the world to search for information.

ویب

2 A **web** is the thin net made by a spider from a string that comes out of its body.

جال

website *noun*

websites

A **website** is a place on the Internet that gives you information.

ویب سائٹ

*Our school has a **website**.*

we'd

1 **We'd** is short for **we had**.

ہم نے (کرلیا)

***We'd** left early in the morning.*

2 **We'd** is also short for **we would**.

ہم (کر چکے ہوں گے)

***We'd** like you to come with us.*

wedding *noun*

weddings

A **wedding** is when two people get married.

شادی

Wednesday *noun*

Wednesdays

Wednesday is the day after Tuesday and before Thursday.

بدھ

week *noun*

weeks

A **week** is a period of seven days.

ہفتہ

*This is the last **week** of the holidays.*

weekend *noun*

weekends

The **weekend** is the days at the end of the week, when you do not go to school or work.

اختتام ہفتہ، ہفتہ اتوار کا دن جب ہفتہ واری چھٹی رہتی ہے

weigh *verb*

weighs, weighing, weighed

If you **weigh** something or someone, you measure how heavy they are.

وزن کرنا

*I **weigh** more than my brother.*

A B C D E F G H I J K L M N O P Q R S T U V W X Y Z

weight *noun*

The **weight** of a person or thing is how heavy they are.

وزن

*What is your **weight** and height?*

well

better, best

If you do something **well**, you do it in a good way.

اچھا

*He draws **well**.*

well *noun*

A **well** is a deep hole in the ground from which people take water, oil or gas.

کنواں

we'll

We'll is short for **we will**.

ہم (کریں گے)

***We'll** come along later.*

went

➪ Look at **go**.

*They **went** to school.*

were

➪ Look at **be**.

*They **were** at home yesterday.*

we're

We're is short for **we are**.

ہم (کر رہے ہیں)

***We're** late!*

weren't

Weren't is short for **were not**.

نہیں تھے

*They **weren't** at school yesterday.*

west *noun*

The **west** is the direction ahead of you when you are looking towards the place where the sun goes down.

مغرب

wet *adjective*

wetter, wettest

If something is **wet**, it is covered in water.

بھیگا، گیلی

we've

We've is short for **we have**.

ہم نے

***We've** got lots of books.*

whale *noun*

whales

Whales are very large sea mammals.

وہیل

***Whales** breathe through a hole on the top of their heads.*

what

You use **what** in questions when you ask for information.

کیا

***What** time is it?*

wheat *noun*

Wheat is a crop. People make flour and bread from **wheat**.

گیہوں

wheel *noun*

wheels

Wheels are round and they turn. Bikes and cars move along on **wheels**.

پہیہ

wheelchair *noun*

wheelchairs

A **wheelchair** is a chair with wheels that you use if you cannot walk.

پہیہ دار کرسی

when

You use **when** to ask what time something happened or will happen.

کب

***When** are you leaving?*

where

You use **where** to ask questions about the place something is in.

کہاں

Where's *your house?*

which

You use **which** when you want help to choose between things.

کون

Which *shoes should I put on?*

while

If one thing happens **while** another thing is happening, the two things are happening at the same time.

جبکہ، دوران

She goes to work ***while*** *her children are at school.*

whisper *verb*

whispers, whispering, whispered

When you **whisper**, you speak in a very quiet voice.

دھیمی آواز سے کچھ کہنا

Don't you know it's rude to ***whisper****?*

whistle *verb*

whistles, whistling, whistled

When you **whistle**, you make sounds like music by blowing hard.

سیٹی، وسل

white *noun*

White is the colour of snow or milk.

سفید

His shirt is ***white****.*

who

You use **who** in questions when you ask about someone's name.

کون

Who *won the quiz?*

who'd

Who'd is short for **who would**.

کون (کرے گا)

Who'd *like to come with me?*

whole *adjective*

The **whole** of something is all of it.

کل، سالم، مکمل، پورا

Have the ***whole*** *cake.*

who'll

Who'll is short for **who will**.

کون (کرے گا)

Who'll *go and find her?*

whose

You use **whose** to ask who something belongs to.

کس کی

Whose *bag is this?*

why

You use **why** when you are asking about the reason for something.

کیوں

Why *did you do it?*

wide *adjective*

wider, widest

Something that is **wide** is a large distance from one side to the other.

وسیع، کشادہ، چوڑا

The bed is too ***wide*** *for this room.*

width *noun*

The **width** of something is the distance from one side to another.

چوڑائی

Measure the full ***width*** *of the table.*

wife *noun*

wives

A man's **wife** is the woman he is married to.

بیوی

wild *adjective*

wilder, wildest

Wild animals or plants live or grow in nature, and people do not take care of them.

جنگلی

will *verb*

You use **will** to talk about things that are going to happen in the future.

کرے گا (مستقبل)

*Mum **will** be angry.*

win *verb*

wins, winning, won

If you **win**, you do better than everyone.

جیتنا

*You've **won** first prize!*

wind *noun*

Wind is air that moves.

ہوا

wind *verb*

winds, winding, wound

1 If a road or river **winds**, it twists and turns.

مڑنا

2 When you **wind** something long around something, you wrap it around several times.

لپیٹنا

*She **wound** the rope around her waist.*

window *noun*

windows

A **window** is a space in the wall of a building or in the side of a vehicle that has glass in it.

کھڑکی

wing *noun*

wings

The **wings** of birds, insects or aeroplanes are the parts that keep them in the air.

بازو، ڈینے

winner *noun*

winners

The **winner** of a race or competition is the person who wins it.

فاتح

*Our teacher will give the prizes to the **winners**.*

winter *noun*

winters

Winter is the season after autumn and before spring. In the **winter** the weather is usually cold.

سردی کا موسم

wipe *verb*

wipes, wiping, wiped

If you **wipe** dirt or liquid from something, you remove it using a cloth or your hands.

پونچھنا

*She **wiped** the tears from her eyes.*

wire *noun*

wires

A **wire** is a long thin piece of metal.

تار

*The birds were sitting on a telephone **wire**.*

wise *adjective*

wiser, wisest

A **wise** person can decide on the right thing to do.

عاقل، فہیم

wish *verb*

wishes, wishing, wished

If you **wish** something, you would like it to be true.

خواہش

*I **wish** I had a pet.*

witch *noun*

witches

In children's stories, a **witch** is a woman who has magic powers that she uses to do bad things.

ساحرہ

with

1 If one person is **with** another, they are together in one place.
ساتھ
*He's watching a film **with** his friends.*

2 You use **with** to say that someone has something.
کے ساتھ
*My daughter is the girl **with** brown hair.*

without

If you do something **without** someone, they are not in the same place as you are, or they are not doing the same thing as you.
بغیر
*He went **without** me.*

wives

⇨ Look at **wife**.
*The men bought flowers for their **wives**.*

wizard *noun*

wizards

In children's stories, a **wizard** is a man who has magic powers.
جادوگر، ساحر

woke

⇨ Look at **wake**.
*They **woke** early.*

woken

⇨ Look at **wake**.
*We were **woken** by a loud noise.*

wolf *noun*

wolves

A **wolf** is a wild animal that looks like a large dog.
بھیڑیا

woman *noun*

women

A **woman** is an adult female person.
عورت

won

⇨ Look at **win**.
*She **won** first prize.*

won't

Won't is short for **will not**.
نہیں کروں گا
*I **won't** be late.*

wood *noun*

woods

1 **Wood** is the hard material that trees are made of.
لکڑی

2 A **wood** is a large area of trees growing near each other.
جنگل

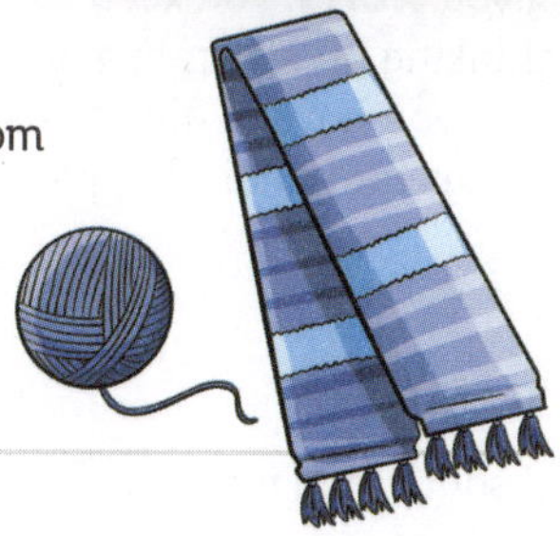

wool *noun*

Wool is a material made from the fur of sheep. It is used for making things such as clothes.
اون

word *noun*

words

Words are things that you say or write.
لفظ
*Some **words** are short and some are long.*

wore

⇨ Look at **wear**.
*She **wore** a red dress.*

work *verb*

works, working, worked

1 When you **work**, you do something that uses a lot of your time or effort.
کام کرنا
*We **work** hard all day.*

2 If a machine **works**, it does its job.
کام کرنا
*The TV isn't **working**.*

a b c d e f g h i j k l m n o p q r s t u v w x y z

world *noun*
worlds
The **world** is the earth, the planet we live on.
دنیا

worm *noun*
worms
A **worm** is a small animal with a long thin body, no bones, and no legs.
کیڑا

worn
⇨ Look at **wear**.
*Have you **worn** this?*

worry *verb*
worries, worrying, worried
If you **worry**, you keep thinking about problems that you have or about nasty things that might happen.
فکر کرنا

worse
If something is **worse** than another thing, it is not as good.
بے کار، برا، خراب
*My spelling is **worse** than yours.*

worst
If something is the **worst**, all other things are better.
سب سے برا
*That was the **worst** day in my life.*

worth
If something is **worth** a sum of money, that's how much you could sell it for.
قیمت، ساکھ
*This gold ring is **worth** a lot of money.*

would *verb*
You use **would** to say that someone agreed to do something. You use **would not** to say that they refused to do something.
کرے گا
*They said they **would** come to my party.*

wound
⇨ Look at **wind**.
*She **wound** the rope around her wrist.*

wrap *verb*
wraps, wrapping, wrapped
When you **wrap** something, you fold paper or cloth around it to cover it.
لپیٹنا
*I didn't have enough paper to **wrap** the present.*

wrist *noun*
wrists
Your **wrist** is the part of your body between your arm and your hand. Your **wrists** bend when you move your hands.
کلائی

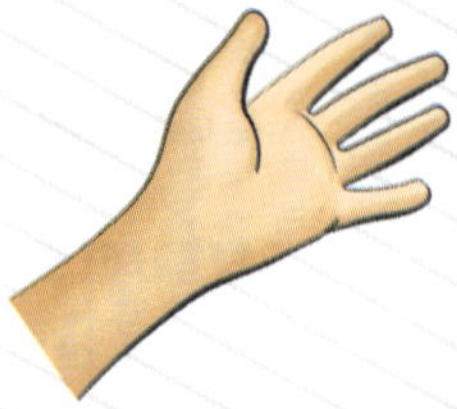

write *verb*
writes, writing, wrote, written
When you **write** something, you use a pen or pencil to make letters, words, or numbers.
لکھنا
*He **wrote** his name in the book.*

writing *noun*
Writing is words that have been written or printed.
تحریر
*Can you read my **writing**?*

written
⇨ Look at **write**.
*My uncle has **written** a song.*

wrong *adjective*
1 If you say that an answer is **wrong**, you mean that it is not right.
غلط، صحیح نہ ہونا
*No, you've got that **wrong**!*
2 If you say that something someone does is **wrong**, you mean that it is bad.
غلط، خراب
*It is **wrong** to hurt animals.*

Xx

X-ray *noun*
X-rays
An **X-ray** is a picture of the inside of someone's body.
ایکسرے
*The **X-ray** showed that my arm was broken.*

xylophone *noun*
xylophones
A **xylophone** is an instrument made of flat pieces of wood or metal in a row. You hit the pieces with a stick to make different sounds.
زائلوفون، چوبی باجہ

Yy

yacht *noun*
yachts
A **yacht** is a large boat with sails or an engine, used for races or for making trips.
پانی کا جہاز

yawn *verb*
yawns, yawning, yawned
If you **yawn**, you open your mouth very wide and breathe in more air than usual because you are tired or bored.
جماہی لینا

year *noun*
years
A **year** is a period of twelve months, beginning on January 1 and finishing on December 31.
سال

yell *verb*
yells, yelling, yelled
If you **yell**, you shout something, often because you are angry.
غصے میں چیخنا، چلانا
*She **yelled** at him to stop.*

yellow *noun*
Yellow is the colour of lemons or butter.
پیلا، زرد
*Her favourite colour is **yellow**.*

yes
You say **yes** to agree with someone or to say that something is true, or if you want something.
ہاں!

yesterday
Yesterday is the day before today.
گزشتہ کل
*There was no school **yesterday**.*

yogurt or **yoghurt** *noun*
yogurts or **yoghurts**
Yogurt is a thick liquid food that is made from milk.
دہی
*I like strawberry **yogurt** more than peach **yogurt**.*

yolk *noun*
yolks
The **yolk** of an egg is the yellow part.
انڈے کی زردی

you
You means the person or people that someone is talking or writing to.
تم، آپ
*Can I help **you**?*

A B C D E F G H I J K L M N O P Q R S T U V W X Y Z

you'd

1 **You'd** is short for **you had**.
آپ نے کیا
*I thought **you'd** told him.*

2 **You'd** is also short for **you would**.
آپ کریں گے
***You'd** like it a lot.*

you'll

You'll is short for **you will**.
آپ کریں گے
***You'll** be late!*

young *adjective*

younger, youngest

A **young** person, animal, or plant has not lived for very long.
نوجوان
*A kitten is a **young** cat.*

your

You use **your** to show that something belongs to the people that you are talking to.
تمہارا، آپ کا
*I do like **your** name.*

you're

You're is short for **you are**.
آپ کر رہے ہیں
***You're** very early!*

yours

Yours refers to something belonging to the people that you are talking to.
آپ کا
*His hair is longer than **yours**.*

yourself

yourselves

Yourself means you alone.
آپ خود
*You'll hurt **yourself**.*

you've

You've is short for **you have**.
***You've** got very long legs.*

Zz

zebra *noun*

zebras

A **zebra** is a wild African animal like a horse with black and white stripes.
زیبرا

zero

zeros or **zeroes**

Zero is the number **0**.
صفر

zip *noun*

zips

A **zip** is two long rows of little teeth and a piece that slides along them. You pull this to open or close the **zip**.
زپ، چین

zoo *noun*

zoos

A **zoo** is a place where live animals are kept so that people can look at them.
چڑیا گھر